Early Childhood

BIG BOOK of Bible Activities, Songs, and Rhymes

DAVID C COOK
transforming lives together

BIG BOOK OF BIBLE ACTIVITIES, SONGS, AND RHYMES FOR EARLY CHILDHOOD
Published by David C Cook
4050 Lee Vance Drive
Colorado Springs, CO 80918 U.S.A.

Integrity Music Limited, a Division of David C Cook
Brighton, East Sussex BN1 2RE, England

ISBN 978-0-8307-7241-4

The content included in this book was originally published in *Bible Songs & Action Rhymes Ages 3–6* by Standard Publishing in 2005 © Standard Publishing, ISBN 10: 0-7847-1781-8.

Cover Design: James Hershberger
Illustrator: Rusty Fletcher

Printed in the United States of America

3 4 5 6 7 8 9 10 11 12

111124

Contents

New Testament

Introduction

Big Book of Bible Activities, Songs, and Rhymes for Early Childhood is designed to make each lesson more fun and interactive for children ages 3–6! With 66 songs, 30 rhymes, and 102 teaching ideas, this book is a great tool for teachers! Each page in this book includes a Scripture reference and Bible story title to help you identify which Bible story the song, rhyme, or idea correlates to (also available in the table of contents). These songs, rhymes, and ideas will keep your kids singing, moving, and actively learning each time they come to class and will help them remember the Bible stories long after they've gone home!

Bible Songs

The Bible songs are piggyback songs written to familiar tunes. Music scores are included in the back of the book for tunes that may be unfamiliar to you.

Action Rhymes

Children learn quickly when they can move and interact with the stories they're learning! The action rhymes in this book include motions that you can do with the children in your class as you learn the rhymes. Practice the motions before class so that you can comfortably lead them as you teach.

Teaching Ideas

Each song and rhyme includes a correlating, creative teaching idea. These ideas offer fun ways to teach the song or rhyme or ways to reinforce the Bible story with the children you teach. Each teaching idea includes a list of supplies you'll need as well as detailed directions. When a craft is involved, examples are shown to help you understand what the activity will look like when it is completed.

Activity Options for Younger Children

These options were designed to help make activities easier for children at the younger range of the early-childhood age level. Adapt the teaching ideas to the age you teach.

Helps

The table of contents is arranged canonically by Scripture references for your convenience. Each listing also tells you if what's listed is a song, rhyme, or teaching idea so that you can find what you're looking for quickly and easily!

The index on pages 218–222 will help you find specific songs, rhymes, and ideas in alphabetical order within each of these three categories.

If you're using HeartShaper Children's Curriculum, you'll want to check out the Scope and Sequence on pages 223–224 to find songs, rhymes, and ideas that correlate to your lesson each week.

God Made

God Made the Sky and Earth; God Made Fish and Birds; God Made Animals; God Made People
Genesis 1

Tune: "Jesus Loves Me"

God made daytime and night too.
God made sunlight and the moon.
God made all the stars at night.
See them twinkle, oh so bright.

Chorus:
God made them all. God made them all.
God made them all. Yes, God made them all.

God made mountains and the hills.
God made grass and daffodils.
God made tasty food to eat—
veggies green and fruit that's sweet.

Repeat chorus

God made bugs and God made birds.
God made fish and cattle herds.
God made every animal—
some are big and some are small.

Repeat chorus

God made dads and mommies too,
brothers, sisters—even you.
Grandmas, Grandpas we can love.
All these blessings from above.

Song suggestion: Because this song contains several verses, consider teaching it to the children over the course of several weeks. Teach one verse each week until the entire song is learned. Sing the song slowly at first while the children are learning the words and then speed up the song as you like once you feel the children can keep up. Adding motions will help kids remember the verses, and the added energy will help keep kids engaged!

Creation Sensory Bottles

God Made the Sky and Earth; God Made Fish and Birds; God Made Animals; God Made People
Genesis 1

Use these Creation Sensory Bottles to help children visualize what God made on each day of creation.

Allow kids to make individual Creation Sensory Bottles or use 2-liter bottles and place them in a learning center for the children to share. Kids can peer at the items through the plastic bottles or shake the bottles to see the items move inside.

Supplies

- small, clear plastic bottles with caps (2-liter bottles to use in a learning center; 3 per child)
- water
- duct tape
- black permanent marker
- glue

Additional Supplies for Days 1–4 of Creation

- 1 large piece of black fabric
- 1 large piece of white fabric
- small pebbles (5 per child or enough to cover the bottom of each bottle)
- small silk flowers (3–5 per child)

Directions for Days 1–4 of Creation

Before class cut the black and white fabric into strips. Each strip should be 3" long and ½" wide. Cut enough for each child to have one black strip and one white strip.

Give each child one clear, plastic bottle. Have the children place the black and white fabric into their bottles as you talk about God making light and dark. Talk about God making the earth and water as the children add pebbles and water to their bottles. Do not fill the bottles completely—leave room to add the flowers. Talk about God making plants as the children add the silk flowers to their bottles. Secure the caps on each bottle using duct tape. Label each bottle with the child's name.

Additional Supplies for Day 5 of Creation

- colorful craft feathers (2 or 3 per child)
- small fish cut from craft foam (3–5 per child)

Directions for Day 5 of Creation

Before class cut out fish from the craft foam that are small enough to fit through the opening of a bottle.

Give each child a new bottle. Have the children place several feathers into their bottles. Talk about God making the birds. When you talk about God making the fish, have the children place the foam fish in their bottles. Finish by adding water to the bottles and securing the caps with duct tape

Additional Supplies for Day 6 of Creation

- small plastic or foam animals (4 per child)

Directions for Day 6 of Creation

Give each child a new bottle. Have the children place the small plastic or foam animals into their bottles. Talk about God making all of the different kinds of animals. Secure the caps with duct tape.

Cake Pan Creation

God Made the Sky and Earth; God Made Fish and Birds; God Made Animals; God Made a World for People

Genesis 1

Have fun making this creation scene with children as you talk about what God made.

Supplies

- 9" x 13" cake pan
- small bag of potting soil
- 3 small houseplants
- 1 cup of water
- 3 or more small, plastic animals

Directions

Ask the children what God created when He made the world. As children respond, begin placing the items listed into the cake pan. First place soil into the pan. Next, add several small houseplants to the soil. Add the water, distributing it evenly around the soil. Finally, place several small, plastic animals in the pan to complete the creation scene.

As you move through this activity, explain to the children that God made the world and prepared a special place where people can live. Consider asking children to tell about their favorite things that God made.

Close with a prayer, thanking God for making a wonderful world for people.

God Made People

God Made People; God Made Adam and Eve
Genesis 1–2

God made Adam and Eve his wife.
(raise pointer finger of right hand for Adam then add middle finger for Eve)

God formed their bodies
(pat arms)

and gave them life.
(cup hands at mouth and blow puff of air)

God gave them legs and feet to walk,
(point to legs; march in place)

eyes to see, and mouths to talk.
(point to eyes then to mouth)

They used their arms to carry things
(flex muscles twice as though lifting weights)

Their ears could hear the bluebirds sing.
(cup hand at ear as though straining to hear something)

God loved the people He made back then.
(cross arms over chest)

He loves us too; He is our friend.
(nod head yes)

Stick People Puppets

God Made People; God Made Adam and Eve
Genesis 1–2; Proverbs 20

Supplies

- assorted pictures of people's heads cut from magazines or taken from the Internet (each about the size of a nickel)
- scissors
- wooden craft sticks (1 per child)
- tape

Directions

Before class cut several pictures of people's heads from old magazines or from pictures taken from the Internet. Kids will attach these to wooden craft sticks to make stick puppets. Each head should be approximately the size of a nickel. Prepare enough for each child to have at least one puppet.

During class assist children in taping precut pictures of people's heads to the ends of craft sticks.

Talk with children about how the people they chose look different from the others that were chosen by the other children. Talk with children about the similarities and differences between people and about how God made each person unique and special.

Encourage the children to put on a puppet show using their Stick People Puppets.

Say a prayer, thanking God for all of the children in the class and for making each person special.

People Puzzles

God Made People; God Made Adam and Eve
Genesis 1–2

Supplies

- white roll paper (enough to trace the outline of 1 child for every 4 children in the class)
- black permanent marker
- scissors
- crayons, washable markers, or dry erase markers
- tape or reusable adhesive

Directions

Before class trace and cut out the outline of a child on a sheet of white roll paper. Cut one paper person for every four children in your class. Cut each figure into several large puzzle pieces: hands, feet, arms, legs, head, and torso. You may want to laminate each figure before cutting it apart to keep the pieces from curling at the edges. If you do this, use dry erase markers for the next step.

During class divide the children into groups of four. Give each group a puzzle and assist the children in coloring and assembling their people puzzles. You may want to allow children to attach their puzzles to a wall using tape or reusable adhesive.

As a class, talk about the purpose of each body part and about how they all work together. Remind the children that God made people special. Close with a prayer, thanking God for making people and for giving us bodies that we can use to serve Him.

Activity Option

For added fun, play a racing game. Put all the puzzle pieces into one pile. Divide the children into four groups. Call out a body part and have one person from each group run and get that body part from the pile and take it back to its group. As body parts are gathered, have children assemble their puzzles.

The Senses

God Made My Senses
Genesis 1–2

Adam saw a smiling face.
(point to eyes and smile)

Eve heard a little giggle.
(cup hand to ear)

Their noses smelled a flower.
(point to nose and sniff)

Their fingers touched and wiggled.
(wiggle fingers)

Their tongues tasted water.
(point to mouth)

They could talk and sing.

Their senses were a special gift,
(nod head yes)

from God, who made all things.
(point up)

My eyes can see a smiling face.
(point to eyes and smile)

My ears can hear a giggle.
(cup hand to ear)

My nose can smell a flower.
(point to nose and sniff)

My fingers touch and wiggle.
(wiggle fingers)

My tongue can lick an ice cream cone.
(point to mouth)

I can talk and sing.

My senses are a special gift,
(nod head yes)

from God, who made all things.
(point up)

Five Senses Discovery Tray

God Made My Senses
Genesis 1–2; Proverbs 20

Supplies

- cookie sheet or metal tray
- various items kids can see, hear, smell, taste, and touch (ideas are listed below):
  see—kaleidoscope, bright scarf, or necktie
  hear—bubble wrap to pop, ticking clock, or music box
  smell—cinnamon stick, spices in plastic bag, or potpourri
  touch—feather, sponge, or sandpaper
  taste—food items (raisins, orange or apple slices, or bread)

Directions

Before you begin, make sure everyone has washed their hands. Place the sensory items on cookie sheet or metal tray. As the children explore each item, talk about what senses are being used and about how each sense is different. Some of the items can use more than one of the senses. Challenge children to think of all of the senses used for each item.

Remind the children that God made our senses and we can use them to learn about the wonderful world He made. Close with prayer, thanking God for making all of our senses.

Remember to confirm whether there are children in your class with allergies. Choose food items appropriately.

God Has Made Me Very Special

God Made Me Special
Genesis 1–2; Psalm 8, 139; Matthew 10

Tune: "I've Been Working on the Railroad"

God has made me very special,
and you are special too.
God has made us very special
with special work to do.
We can care for friends and neighbors,
for pets and family too.
God has made us very special
with special work to do.

Thumbing Special Cards

God Made Me Special
Genesis 1–2; Psalm 8, 139; Matthew 10

Supplies

- 8½" x 11" paper (preferably white, 1 sheet per child)
- washable stamp pads in assorted colors
- crayons or washable markers
- moist towelettes

Directions

Before class fold sheets of paper in half. Make one card for each child in your class. On the front of each card write "You Are Thumbing Special."

During class tell the children they will be making cards for someone special. They may choose a family member, church member, or a friend. Some children may not be able to decide on just one special person, so be prepared to distribute additional cards if needed.

Assist the children in making thumbprints by pressing their thumbs into the washable stamp pads and then onto the insides of their cards. Help the children sign their names inside their cards. Allow children to decorate their cards using crayons or washable markers.

Mr. Noah Built an Ark

Noah Builds a Boat; Noah and the Flood
Genesis 6–9

Tune: "This Old Man"

Mr. Noah built an ark—
built it out of gopher bark.
With a *zzz*, *smack*, give a *whack*,
build a floating zoo.
God helped Noah—He'll help you.

Mr. Noah built a boat—
smeared with tar to make it float.
With a *zzz*, *smack*, give a *whack*,
build a floating zoo.
God helped Noah—He'll help you.

Mr. Noah searched to find
animals of every kind.
With a *zzz*, *smack*, give a *whack*,
build a floating zoo.
God helped Noah—He'll help you.

Mr. Noah felt a drop—
rained 40 days and didn't stop.
With a *zzz*, *smack*, give a *whack*,
build a floating zoo.
God helped Noah—He'll help you.

Mr. Noah parked the boat.
The land was dry—it would not float.
With a *zzz*, *smack*, give a *whack*,
build a floating zoo.
God helped Noah—He'll help you.

Mr. Noah spied a sight—
a rainbow bright with colored light.
God saved animals,
and Noah's family.
He helped Noah—He'll help me.

Noah Sound and Movement

Noah Builds a Boat; Noah and the Flood
Genesis 6–9

Supplies

- "Mr. Noah Built an Ark" Bible song (p. 18)
- toy tools
- wood blocks

Directions

Give children toy tools and allow them to act out building the ark. Remind children that the ark was very large. Encourage children to act out stretching high and far to reach each area of the ark as they build.

Teach the children the Bible song "Mr. Noah Built an Ark." Have children use toy saws when they make the zzz noise. Those with wood blocks can hit them together when they come to the word *smack*. Children with hammers can pretend to hammer nails in place when they say the word *whack*.

Teach the song slowly. Each time you repeat the song, allow children to trade tools with one another so that they can act out a different part of the song. As children become familiar with the song, try speeding up the words to see how fast you can sing without missing words.

Rainbow Names

Noah Builds a Boat; Noah and the Flood
Genesis 6–9

Make these colorful name creations to remind children that a rainbow is a sign of God's promise to care for all people and never to flood the whole earth again.

Supplies

- copy of the Rainbow Names pattern (p. 210; 1 per child)
- fruit flavored, colorful, O-shaped cereal (1 handful per child, extra for eating!)
- liquid glue
- paper towels or moist towelettes

Directions

Before class make one copy of the Rainbow Names pattern page for each child. Clearly print each child's name on his or her paper using large uppercase and lowercase letters.

Give each child a handful of the fruit flavored, colorful, O-shaped cereal. Help each child glue the cereal over the printed letters of his name. As children work on this activity, explain to them that God promised to care for each one of us by not flooding the whole earth again.

Explain that the rainbow in the sky was a sign from God to remind all of us of His special promise. The rainbow colors on their names can remind children that a rainbow is a sign of God's promise to care for all people and never to flood the whole earth again.

Tell children God's love is like a circle that never ends. Show them a piece of the O-shaped cereal and point out that the circle never stops. God's love for each one of us will never end either.

Remember to have paper towels or moist towelettes nearby for messy fingers.

Abram Pack

Abram Moves
Genesis 12

Tune: "Did You Ever See a Lassie"

Oh, Abram pack your suitcase, your suitcase, your suitcase.
Oh, Abram pack your suitcase, for it's moving day.
Pack your donkeys and camels.
Pack your carts up till they're full.
Oh, Abram pack your suitcase, for it's moving day.

Oh, Abram pack your suitcase, your suitcase, your suitcase.
Oh, Abram pack your suitcase, for it's moving day.
You're moving to a new land.
We'll lend you a helping hand.
Oh, Abram pack your suitcase, for it's moving day.

Pack a Pak

Abram Moves
Genesis 12

Supplies

- personal items (miscellaneous toiletries, clothing items, etc., that one might pack when moving or going on a trip)
- old suitcase

Directions

Before class collect several personal items a person might pack when moving or going on a trip. Items could include toiletries, clothing items, or other personal belongings. Try to collect enough items for each child in the class to pack one or two in the suitcase.

During class let each child place one or two items in the suitcase as the class sings the Bible song "Abram Pack" (p. 21). After the song, unpack the items and start again, allowing children to exchange items to pack.

Talk with the children about moving. Ask if any children in your class have ever moved anywhere with their families. Talk about the sadness of leaving one place and about the excitement of going to a new place. Explore feelings that Abram and his family might have had when they left their home to go to a new land.

Close with a prayer, thanking God for caring for us everywhere we go.

Abram Chose to Be Fair

Abram and Lot
Genesis 13

Tune: "Did You Ever See a Lassie?"

Oh, Abram chose to be fair, to be fair, to be fair.
Oh, Abram chose to be fair and do right all the time.
Oh, be fair and do right; yes, be fair and do right.
Oh, Abram chose to be fair and do right all the time.

Oh, we will choose to be fair, to be fair, to be fair.
Oh, we will choose to be fair and do right all the time.
Oh, be fair and do right; yes, be fair and do right.
Oh, we will choose to be fair and do right all the time.

Additional verses:
We will choose to be kind.
We will choose to make peace.
We will choose to take turns.
We will choose to help out.

Telling Hearts Game

Abram and Lot
Genesis 13

Supplies

- "Abram Chose to Be Fair" Bible song (p. 23)
- red card stock
- scissors
- clear contact paper or packing tape

Directions

Before class cut several medium-sized hearts from red card stock. Cover the hearts with clear contact paper or packing tape to make them more durable.

During class teach the children the Bible song "Abram Chose to Be Fair." Sit in a circle with the children. As you sing the song, pass several hearts around the circle. Stop passing the hearts at the end of the first verse. Each child left holding a heart should try to tell one way he or she can be fair. If children have trouble thinking of ways to be fair, offer examples of situations where they could chose to be fair or to be selfish. Help them chose the right answer and tell how they can be fair in that situation.

Sing the second verse, passing the hearts in the opposite direction around the circle this time. Repeat the activity at the end of the second verse with different children telling how they can be fair.

Sing additional verses, allowing children to name ways they can be kind, make peace, take turns, and help out.

Talk with the children about how Abram chose to be fair when he allowed Lot to choose his land first. Close with a prayer, asking God to help you know how to be fair in each situation.

Abraham and Sarah

Abraham and Sarah Have a Baby

Genesis 17–18, 21

Tune: "Eensy Weensy Spider"

Abraham and Sarah were very old and sad.
They didn't have a child to hold or make them glad.
God told them something that brought them both great joy.
He would send them Isaac, a little baby boy.

Abraham was happy, and Sarah was glad too.
God kept His promise; His word to them was true.
Little baby Isaac was sent by God above,
And Abraham and Sarah gave Isaac lots of love.

Sad and Glad Faces

Abraham and Sarah Have a Baby
Genesis 17–18, 21

Supplies

- "Abraham and Sarah" Bible song (p. 25)
- small, white paper plates (1 per child)
- crayons or washable markers
- wooden craft sticks (1 per child)
- clear packing tape

Directions

Help each child draw a sad face on one side of a small, white paper plate. Then turn the plate over and draw a happy face on the other side. Attach a craft stick to the bottom of the sad face with packing tape.

Teach the children the Bible song "Abraham and Sarah." Encourage children to show the sad faces when they sing about Abraham and Sarah being sad and the happy faces when they sing about Abraham and Sarah being glad.

Joseph as a Boy

Joseph as a Boy
Genesis 37, 39

God cared for Joseph, in good times and in bad.
(point both thumbs up and then down)

God cared for Joseph, and that made Joseph glad.
(nod head yes and smile)

When trouble came to Joseph, he did not hide his head.
(shake head no)

He prayed to God in heaven and trusted what God said.
(place hands together as though praying)

When trouble comes upon you, do not run away.
(shake head no)

God cares for you all the time, just turn to Him and pray.
(point out; then hands together as though praying)

Praying Hands

Joseph as a Boy

Genesis 37, 39

Supplies

- white paper
- crayons or washable markers

Directions

Trace one of each child's hands on white paper, leaving space above the hands to write "God cares for me all the time." Help the child think of ways God cares for him or her. Once children have thought of something, help them draw pictures of those places or times inside the outline of their traced hands.

Keep several pieces of extra paper nearby for children who want to start over.

Close with prayer, thanking God for taking care of us all of the time.

Joseph Pleased God

Joseph Serves God All His Life
Genesis 39, 41–42, 45, 47

Tune: "Happy Birthday"

Joseph pleased God and worked hard.
Joseph pleased God and worked hard.
Joseph pleased God and worked hard.
He always did his best!

When things went right or wrong,
when things went right or wrong,
when things went right or wrong,
he always did his best!

Joseph helped his family.
Joseph helped his family.
Joseph helped his family.
He always did his best!

Always trust God and work hard.
Always trust God and work hard.
Always trust God and work hard.
Like Joseph, do your best!

Word Flip

Joseph Serves God All His Life

Genesis 39, 41–42, 45, 47

Supplies

- "Joseph Pleased God" Bible song (p. 29)
- 3 manila folders
- scissors
- black permanent marker

Directions

Before class cut three manila folders in half along the fold so that you have six separate halves. Lay the folders in a row and write "He Always Did His Best!" on the folders (one word on each folder half—the exclamation point should be on the last folder by itself).

Turn the folder halves over and write "Like Joseph, Do Your Best!" on the back of each half (one word on each folder half—the exclamation point should be on the last folder by itself). Make sure that the first words of each sentence are back to back and so on.

Choose six children from the class to hold the word cards while you sing the Bible song "Joseph Pleased God." When you come to the last line of each verse, point out the words on the word cards, one at a time.

On the last verse of the song, indicate to the card holders that they should flip their cards over to the other side to show the last sentence.

Point to the words on the cards each time you sing them. Repeat the song with new volunteers as many times as you like.

Moses in a Basket

Moses Is Born
Exodus 2

Tune: "A-Tisket, A-Tasket"

A tisket, a tasket, there floats a little basket.
A tiny homemade baby crib,
and in it baby Moses hid.
A tisket, a tasket—it's Moses in a basket.

A tisket, a tasket, his mother made a basket.
His sister watched the basket boat.
Oh, where would baby Moses float?
A tisket, a tasket—the princess found the basket.

A tisket, a tasket, God watched the little basket.
God watches over us each day,
when we're asleep or when we play.
A tisket, a tasket—God watched the little basket.

Pass the Basket

Moses Is Born
Exodus 2

Supplies

- "Moses in a Basket" Bible song (p. 31)
- small basket
- small doll wrapped in cloth

Directions

During class teach the children the Bible song "Moses in a Basket." Seat the children in a circle and place the doll in the basket. Talk with the children about how Moses' mother placed him in a basket to try to keep him safe.

As you sing the song, pass the basket and doll around the circle. At the end of each verse, stop passing and see who is left holding the doll and basket. That person should be given an opportunity to tell the class one way God cares for us. If the children have trouble thinking of things, help them remember the things they need and have (for example, food, clothes, a home, a loving family, and so on). Continue singing and passing until the song is finished.

Pillar of God

Moses Leads God's People
Exodus 3, 7–13

Tune: "I See the Moon"

Pillar of God in the air
is a sign of God's constant care.
By day it leads and we will go
on the path that God will show.

Pillar of fire in the air
is a sign of God's constant care.
By night it leads to where God shows
the place we'll rest our weary toes.

Pillar Parade

Moses Leads God's People

Exodus 3, 7–13

Supplies

- "Pillar of God" Bible song (p. 33)
- yardstick
- double-sided tape
- yellow card stock
- orange card stock(1 sheet)
- red card stock (1 sheet)
- package of cotton stuffing
- hot-glue gun and 1 or 2 glue sticks
- scissors

Directions

Before class construct a two-sided pillar.

On one side create a pillar of fire to represent God guiding the Israelites at night. Cut yellow poster board in the shape of a flame. Using orange and red construction paper, cut flames that are smaller than the one cut from the yellow poster board. Tape the smaller orange and red flames to the yellow poster board flame. Attach the finished flame to one end of a yardstick using double-sided tape.

On the back of the pillar of fire, make a pillar of cloud to represent God guiding the Israelites by day. Glue cotton stuffing onto the back of the yellow poster board flame using a hot-glue gun.

During class, choose one child to be the leader. This child will hold the two-sided pillar while the other children line up behind him or her. Sing the song "Pillar of God" while the children march around the room. The leader should turn the pillar around when the verse changes from day to night. Repeat this activity choosing a new child to be the leader each time.

Remind the children that God was with the Israelites during the day and at night. Remind the children that God is still with us today.

Activity Option

Allow each child to make a two-sided pillar. Replace the yardstick with wooden craft sticks (one for each child). Give each child a pattern to trace for the flames and use yellow, orange, and red construction paper or card stock. Use liquid glue instead of a hot-glue gun. You will also need scissors for each child. The children can take their pillars home and use them over and over as they sing the "Pillar of God" Bible song.

Moses at the Sea

God's People Cross the Red Sea
Exodus 13–14

Moses led the people as they marched out to the sea.
(march in place)

It looked as if they all were trapped;
(hand over eyes as though searching)

no way they could go free.
(shake head no)

But mighty God in heaven
(point up)

knows all and had a plan.
(point to temple on side of head)

He'd part the sea and make a path—
(move arms apart; point straight ahead)

walk through it on dry land.
(march in place)

I'm sure that it was scary,
(nod head yes)

but when they were afraid, God helped His people cross the sea,
(move arms apart)

and He'll help us be brave.
(point to self)

Smiling Face Sun Catchers

God's People Cross the Red Sea

Exodus 13–14

Supplies

- clear plastic tupperware lids like (1 per child)
- hole punch
- black permanent marker
- several yellow permanent markers
- 6" length of yarn for each child (any color)

Directions

Before class punch a hole near one edge of each lid—this will be the top of the sun catcher. Using a black permanent marker, write "God Helps Us" along the bottom edge of each lid. Draw two eyes and a mouth to make a smiling face on each lid.

During class give each child a yellow permanent marker and a lid. Help the children color the back of their lids using the yellow markers. Allow time for the lids to dry after they've been colored.

Tie a piece of yarn through the hole at the top of each lid to make a sun catcher that can be hung in a window.

Talk with the children about how God is always with us and can help us when we are afraid. Tell them to take the sun catchers home and to hang them in a window as a reminder that God helps us all the time

God Gives to Us

God Provides for His People
Exodus 16–17

Tune: "Old MacDonald Had a Farm"

God gives to us what we need—
food, drink, clothes, home, friends.
God gives to us what we need—
food, drink, clothes, home, friends.
What we eat and what we wear,
a place to live and family.
God gives to us what we need—
food, drink, clothes, home, friends.

Want or Need

God Provides for His People

Exodus 16–17

Supplies

- "God Gives to Us" Bible song (p. 37)
- piece of fruit (real or plastic)
- plastic cup
- item of clothing
- small dollhouse or a picture of a house
- several dolls or picture of a family or a group of friends

Directions

Talk with the children about the difference between wanting something and needing something. Help the children list things that are wanted and things that are needed. As children name things that are listed in the supplies list above, hand out those items. When all of the items have been distributed, ask the children holding an item to come to the front of the class.

Teach the Bible song "God Gives to Us." As each item is mentioned in the song, the child holding that item should hold it up for the class to see. Repeat the song, allowing all of the children to have a turn at holding up an item.

Close with a prayer, thanking God for knowing what we need and giving those things to us.

On Top of Mount Sinai

God Gives Ten Rules
Exodus 19–20, 24, 32

Tune: "On Top of Old Smokey"

On top of Mount Sinai,
God wrote down His law.
On two big stone tablets,
He wrote them for all.

Ten rules He had written
for His people that day.
Those rules can still help us
if we just obey.

God's Top Ten

God Gives Ten Rules

Exodus 19–20, 24, 32

Supplies

- "On Top of Mount Sinai" Bible song (p. 39)

Directions

Teach the children the Bible song "On Top of Mount Sinai." As you sing the song, hold up one finger each time you see an (x) appear in the song (see below for this indication). Continue until all ten fingers are held up at the end of the song. This is a reminder for children about the Ten Commandments given by God.

On Top of Mount Sinai
Tune: "On Top of Old Smokey"

On top of Mount Sinai (x),
God wrote down His law (x).
On two (x x) big stone tablets,
He wrote them for all (x).

Ten rules He had written (x)
for His people that day (x).
Those rules (x) can still help (x) us
if we just obey (x).

Let's Cross over the Jordan

Joshua and Caleb
Numbers 13–14

Tune: "Take Me Out to the Ball Game"

Let's cross over the Jordan.
The land we spied is first rate.
Tasty figs and big clusters of grapes,
milk and honey flow—
Wow, it's so great!
For it's root, root, root for the two spies.
Josh and Caleb said, "Go!"
But the other ten spies that went
answered, "No! No! No!"

Food Container Shakers

Joshua and Caleb
Numbers 13–14

Supplies
- "Let's Cross over the Jordan" Bible song (p. 41)
- assorted empty containers (small potato chip cans, margarine tubs, plastic jars, etc.)
- unpopped popcorn kernels
- clear packing tape

Directions
Before class place several popcorn kernels inside each container. Close the lids tightly and tape the containers closed.

During class teach the children the Bible song "Let's Cross over the Jordan." Give the containers to the children. Let the children use the shakers as they sing the song.

Repeat the song several times, each time allowing different children to shake the containers.

Talk with children about how Joshua and Caleb believed God would help them and take care of them even when others didn't think so. Close with prayer, thanking God for taking good care of us.

Activity Option
For extra fun, cover the containers with white contact paper and allow children to decorate, using glitter markers.

Be Brave and Strong, Joshua

God's People Cross the Jordan River
Joshua 1, 3–4

Tune: "Billy Boy"

Oh, be brave and be strong, Joshua, Joshua.
Oh, be brave and be strong, Joshua.
You need not be afraid,
for the Lord God goes with you.
He will lead you, so obey Him and be true.

Oh, be brave and be strong, boys and girls,
boys and girls.
Oh, be brave and be strong, boys and girls.
You need not be afraid,
for the Lord God goes with you.
He will lead you, so obey Him and be true.

Signs of Bravery and Strength

God's People Cross the Jordan River

Joshua 1, 3–4

Supplies

- "Be Brave and Be Strong, Joshua" Bible song (p. 43)

Directions

To help the children in your class learn the song "Be Brave and Be Strong, Joshua," teach them the sign language for the words *brave* and *strong* (see images). Using their bodies to act out the words in the song will help them learn the words and stay involved in the song.

For the word *brave*, children should place both hands flat against their chests so that their fingertips are touching near their shoulders. They should then pull their hands forward and away from their bodies forcefully while each hand forms a fist position (or the sign for the letter S). See the example below.

Brave

For the word *strong*, children should form the letter S (like a fist) with both hands. The hands should start at the chest and should be pulled firmly away from the body. See the example below.

Strong

You will notice that the signs for the words brave and strong are very similar. A key distinction is that the sign for the word *brave* starts with the hands open, whereas, the sign for the *word* strong begins in the fist position.

Help children practice the signs several times before using them in the song. Sing the song slowly as children try adding in the signs as they sing.

The Walls of Jericho

The Fall of Jericho
Joshua 6

Tune: "The Farmer in the Dell"

The walls of Jericho
were very strong and stout,
but tumbled down when marched around
with trumpet blows and shouts.

At first the walls were up,
and then they tumbled down,
when Joshua and the Israelites
marched seven times around.

What a Blast

The Fall of Jericho
Joshua 6

Children can make their own horns to use when reenacting the story of the fall of Jericho.

Supplies
- crayons or washable markers
- construction paper cut into 8½" squares in a variety of light colors
- tape
- decorative embellishments of your choice

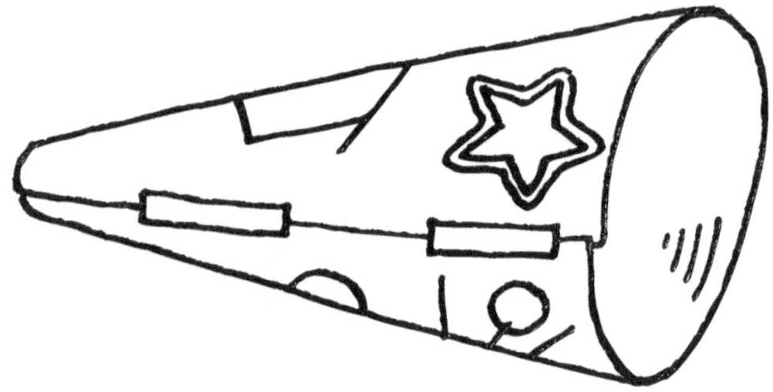

Directions
For this activity the children will decorate a sheet of construction paper as they choose. Allow children to use crayons or washable markers for this activity. Children can also add decorative stickers and other embellishments to make their horns even more fun.

Help the children roll their paper into the shape of a horn. Tape the horns closed at the seams. You will have to round the edge of the horn.

As a group, form a circle and march around the room seven times. Children can count together each time they go around the room. On the final trip around, the children can pretend to blow their horns and shout, "God is mighty!"

The Choice

Joshua Talks to God's People

Joshua 24

Joshua gathered all the people
(motion toward self)

and spoke so all could hear.
(cup hands at mouth; hand to ear as though listening)

He told how God had helped them
(point up)

for many, many years.
(nod head yes)

When Joshua had finished,

he said, "Now make a choice."
(move arms apart; point straight ahead)

walk through it on dry land.
(place hands on hips)

"We will serve the Lord always!"
(cup hands at mouth)

they answered with one voice.
(nod head yes)

Will you serve the Lord today—
(point out)

love Him and follow too?
(cross arms over chest)

The choice is yours to make, my friends.
(point out)

Serve God in all you do.
(point up)

Serve the Lord Memory Game

Joshua Talks to God's People
Joshua 24

Supplies
- index cards
- black permanent marker

Directions
Before class prepare two sets of five index cards to be used in a memory game. Write the words "We will serve the Lord." on the index cards so one word appears on each card. Make a second identical set. You should have ten cards when you are finished.

Play this memory game with a small group of children. Mix up the cards so that they are not in any particular order. Place all cards facedown on the floor or on a low table where children can see and reach the cards. Have the children take turns turning over two cards each. If the words match, they may leave the cards facing up. If the words do not match, they should turn the cards so that they are facing down again. Each child should have one turn at turning over a pair of cards. Continue playing until all of the cards have been matched and you can create the sentence, "We will serve the Lord."

Option for Younger Children
Instead of using words on the two sets of cards, use drawings of a hand, eye, ear, mouth, and foot. Make two identical sets of the five cards. Play the game as directed above, with children searching for matching body parts instead of matching words. As they match the parts, talk with the children about how each part can serve the Lord. For example: my hands can pick up toys; my feet can take me to church; my lips can pray for the sick and sing to God; my eyes can look for people to greet; my ears can hear my parent's words and help me to obey. Continue playing until all of the cards have been matched.

Blow and Shout, Gideon

Gideon Leads God's Army
Judges 6–7

Tune: "London Bridge Is Falling Down"

Blow your trumpets, shout for the Lord,
shout for the Lord, shout for the Lord.
Blow your trumpets, shout for the Lord,
and for Gideon.

He was weak but God is strong,
God is strong, God is strong.
He was weak but God is strong.
Be strong, Gideon.

Gideon's Torch

Gideon Leads God's Army
Judges 6–7

These colorful torches help children visualize the Bible story and have fun reenacting the events.

Supplies

- brown construction paper cut into an 8½" square for each child
- ½ sheet of red tissue paper for each child
- ½ sheet of yellow tissue paper for each child
- clear tape
- stapler
- scissors

Directions

Help the children roll their construction paper squares into a cone shape and secure them with tape. Insert the red and yellow tissue paper into the large, open end of the cones to resemble fire. Tape or staple the tissue paper to the inside of the cones to secure them in place. Trim the tissue paper at the top to make it look more like flames.

Using the torches, children can reenact the story of Gideon leading God's army as they march around the room and shout, "For the Lord and for Gideon!"

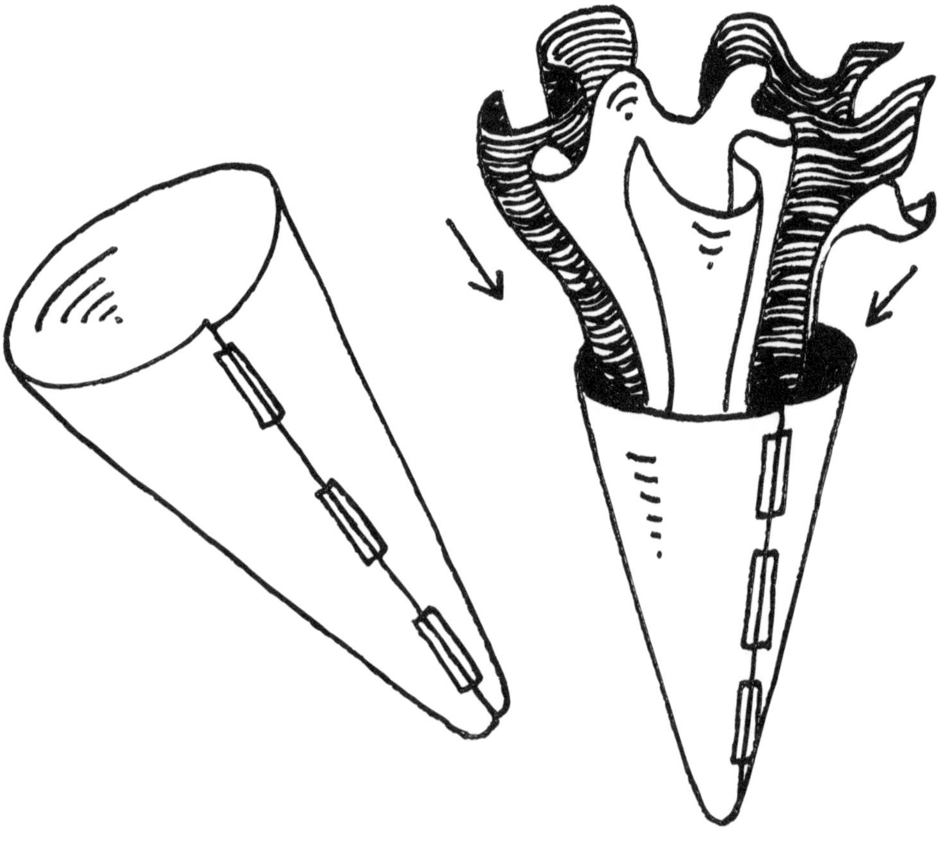

Ruth, a Woman Kind and Smart

Ruth Makes Good Choices
Ruth 1–2

Tune: "Twinkle, Twinkle, Little Star"

Ruth, a woman kind and smart,
made good choices from the start.
She helped Naomi work the land
and married Boaz, a godly man.
Ruth, a woman kind and smart,
made good choices from the start.

Heart Puzzles

Ruth Makes Good Choices

Ruth 1–2

Kids will have fun singing the Bible song "Ruth, a Woman Kind and Smart" while they complete this activity.

Supplies

- the Bible song "Ruth, a Woman Kind and Smart" (p. 51)
- red construction paper cut into heart shapes (one heart for every 2 children)
- scissors
- black permanent marker
- clear contact paper

Directions

Before class, cut out hearts, one heart for every two children. Write the word *good* on the left side of each heart and write the word *choice* on the right side of each heart. Laminate each heart half if possible or use clear contact paper. Cut each heart in half so that no two hearts are cut exactly alike.

As the children enter, give each child half of a heart. Teach the children the Bible song "Ruth, a Woman Kind and Smart" and sing through it several times.

Explain to the children that the next time you sing the song, they are to move around the room and search for the person who has the matching half of their hearts.

Talk with the children about how God wants us to be like Ruth by making good choices. Close with prayer, asking God to help you and the children make good choices.

O Dear Hannah

Samuel as a Boy
1 Samuel 1–3

Tune: "O Suzannah"

O, Samuel, Hannah's son,
was growing up so tall.
His robe no longer fit him right,
for now it was too small.

Chorus
Hannah took good fabric,
a needle and strong thread.
She made a bigger robe for him
to wear around instead.

When Hannah saw her little son,
she ran to give a kiss.
"I've made a robe for you, my child,
and you I really miss."

Repeat chorus

O, Samuel said, "I thank you, Mom,
for all your care and love."
And after thanking Hannah,
then he thanked his God above.

Needle Knockers

Samuel as a Boy
1 Samuel 1–3

Supplies

- "O Dear Hannah" Bible song (p. 53)
- wooden craft sticks (2 per child)
- washable markers

Directions

Give each child two craft sticks and a washable marker. Help the children draw an oval at one end of each craft stick to create the eye of a needle. Use the pretend needles as you sing the Bible song "O Dear Hannah." Show the children how to tap their pretend needles together with the beat of the song. Use the pretend needles as rhythm sticks for the song.

Talk with children about what it's like to get new clothes. Ask how Samuel might have felt when his mother brought him the new clothes she made for him.

Close with prayer, thanking God for families that take good care of us and give us the things we need.

Samuel Served the Lord

Samuel Serves God All His Life
1 Samuel 3, 8–10, 12

Samuel served the Lord when he was very small.
(place palms facing each other with a little space between)

Samuel served the Lord when he grew big and tall.
(make space bigger between hands)

Samuel served the Lord his whole life through.
(make short and then tall signs with hands)

I can serve the Lord my whole life too.
(nod head yes)

Samuel listened hard to hear God's voice.
(cup hand at ear as though listening)

Samuel always tried his best to make the right choice.
(nod head yes)

I can do my best to follow God each day.
(point up)

I can love and serve Him when I work and when I play.
(point to self; nod head yes)

Growing in the Lord Growth Chart

Samuel Serves God All His Life

1 Samuel 3, 8–10, 12

By making these growth charts, kids will be reminded that no one is ever too little or too big to serve God.

Supplies

- white roll paper
- black permanent marker
- measuring tape
- crayons or washable markers
- rubber bands

Directions

Before class cut a sheet of white roll paper that is three to four feet long and one foot wide for each child in the class. At the top of each sheet write "Growing in the Lord."

During class measure each child's height using a measuring tape. You may want the children to remove their shoes prior to measuring. Mark the height of each child on his personal growth chart. Allow the children to draw pictures on their charts showing themselves serving God.

At the end of class, roll up the charts and send them home with the children. You may also want to attach a note encouraging parents to measure their child's growth monthly and to record it on the charts. Each time they measure, the child can add a new picture of himself serving God. By making these growth charts, kids will be reminded that no one is ever too little or too big to serve God.

David Plays the Harp

David Plays for Saul
1 Samuel 16

David plays the harp by strumming on the strings.
(pretend to strum a harp)

David plays the harp. I wonder if he sings?
(place finger on temple as though thinking)

David plays the harp to comfort Saul the king.
(place pretend crown on head)

David plays the harp like it's his favorite thing.
(nod head yes and smile)

Shoe Box Lid Harps

David Plays for Saul
1 Samuel 16

Children can play these harps as a reminder that David used his talent to serve others, and we can do the same.

Supplies

- shoebox lid for every 3 children
- rubber bands of various widths

Directions
Before class assemble the shoe box lid harps by stretching three rubber bands of varying widths across the width of each lid. The widest rubber bands will have the lowest pitch when plucked.

During class allow children to pluck or strum the rubber bands on the shoe box lid harps. Encourage the children to take turns in small groups playing the harps.

Talk with the children about how David used his talent of playing an instrument to serve King Saul. Tell the children when we do something to serve others, we are also serving God.

D.A.V.I.D.

David Meets Goliath
1 Samuel 17

Tune: "Bingo!"

There was a king who liked to sing
and David was his name, oh.
D.A.V.I.D., D.A.V.I.D., D.A.V.I.D.,
and David was his name, oh!

He killed a giant with a sling
and David was his name, oh.
D.A.V.I.D., D.A.V.I.D., D.A.V.I.D.,
and David was his name, oh!

Give Me a D!

David Meets Goliath
1 Samuel 17

Supplies

- Bible song "D.A.V.I.D." (p. 59)
- 5 sheets of white or light colored card stock
- black permanent marker
- clear contact paper

Directions

Before class write each letter of David's name on a separate sheet of card stock. Use all capital letters. Cover each letter card with clear contact paper or laminate them if possible.

During class teach the children the Bible song "D.A.V.I.D." Once the children have learned the song, choose five volunteers to come to the front of the class. Give each volunteer one card with a letter from David's name and line up the children in order. Explain to each child holding a card what letter is on his or her card.

Sing through the song again. This time each child holding a card should hold up his or her card when his or her letter is sung then lower the card after the letter has been sung.

Repeat the song so that each child in the class has a turn to hold a letter card.

I Want to Be a Friend Like Jonathan

David and Jonathan
1 Samuel 18, 20

Tune: "I'm a Little Teapot"

I want to be a friend like Jonathan.
He was loyal to the end.
I want to be a friend like Jonathan.
David could depend on him.

I want to be a friend like King David.
He was loyal to his friend.
I want to be a friend like King David.
He was a friend to Jonathan.

Friendship Chain

David and Jonathan
1 Samuel 18, 20

Children will have fun making these Friendship Chains as reminders to be thankful for their special friends.

Supplies

- light colored construction paper
- crayons or washable markers
- tape

Directions

Before class cut several strips of construction paper so that each child can have one or two strips. Each strip should be 1½" wide and 12" long.

During class assist each child in writing the name of a special friend on a strip of paper. Some children may want to write more than one name. Have several extra precut strips on hand.

Join the strips together to form a friendship chain by taping each strip at the ends with the name of the special friend showing on the outside of the loop.

Hang the finished Friendship Chain in the classroom as a reminder to be thankful for our special friends.

Option for Younger Children

Allow younger children who are unable to write to draw pictures of their special friends on their strips. Each child may want to draw just the face of their friend since the strips are narrow. Consider cutting wider strips ahead of time if you think that some children will want to draw instead of write. A strip that is 2½" or 3" wide will allow adequate space for drawing.

God Wants Us to Be Kind

David and Mephibosheth
2 Samuel 9

Tune: "Mary Had a Little Lamb"

David helped Mephibosheth,
Mephibosheth, Mephibosheth.
David helped Mephibosheth.
He was very kind.

David gave him food to eat,
food to eat, food to eat.
David gave him food to eat.
He was very kind.

God wants us to help others,
help others, help others.
God wants us to help others,
help others and be kind.

David's Table

David and Mephibosheth
2 Samuel 9

Supplies

- copy of the David's Table crown (p. 211; 1 per child)
- construction paper
- crayons or washable markers
- tape
- healthy snacks for the class

Directions

Before class cut the construction paper into strips that are 1" wide and 12" long. Make sure you have enough so that each child in the class can have one. You may want to prepare extras in case some tear.

During class help children color and cut out the crowns. Tape a strip of construction paper to one side of each crown and size the crown to fit the child's head. Tape the other end of the construction paper strip to the opposite side of the crown to make a headband so that the crown can be worn.

Choose a few children to serve the snack. Make sure everyone has washed their hands. Use this time to reenact the story of David inviting Mephibosheth to eat at his table. The children serving the snacks can invite the other children to come and sit at the table. The children serving should wear their crowns as they pretend to be King David. The children being served can remove their crowns (although most will probably want to wear theirs).

As the children pass out the snacks, talk about how David showed kindness to Mephibosheth by inviting him to eat at King David's table.

When it is time to clean up, ask the children who were served at the beginning of snack time to help clean up. They can put on their crowns as they pretend to be King David.

End with prayer, asking God to help you and the children find ways to show kindness to others.

Remember to check with parents for any food allergies before serving snacks.

David Sings to God

David Sings to God
2 Samuel 22; Psalm 4–5, 23, 100, 122, 150

Tune: "The Farmer in the Dell"

David sings to God.
David sings to God.
When he's glad or when he's sad,
David sings to God.

David sings to God.
David sings to God.
God's power and might at day or night,
David sings to God.

We can sing to God.
We can sing to God.
When we're glad or when we're sad,
we can sing to God.

We can sing to God.
We can sing to God.
Our thanks and love to Him above,
we can sing to God.

Sing and Share

David Sings to God

2 Samuel 22; Psalm 4–5, 23, 100, 122, 150

Share these with others who could benefit from the encouragement of young children singing praises to God.

Supplies

- computer or smart phone with recording abilities
- blank CD or flash drive

Directions

Record the children singing their favorite songs about God as a group or individually. Record as many songs as possible on a computer or smart phone. You may want to add to this recording over several weeks.

When the recording is complete make several copies to send to nursing home residences. Make copies by by burning the recordings onto a blank CD or copy the files onto a flash drive. If you used a phone to record, you will have to upload the files to your computer before you can make copies. Consider emailing the files as an alternative.

Talk with the children about how singing praises to God pleases Him and can also encourage others.

Activity Option

If you plan to send hard copies to nursing homes, consider allowing the children to make cards to go along with them.

Be My Helper

Solomon Prays to Know What Is Right
1 Kings 3–4

Tune: "Clementine"

Be my helper, be my helper,
be my helper all day long.
Be my helper God in heaven
as I'm choosing right from wrong.

Be my helper, be my helper,
be my helper day and night.
Be my helper God in heaven
help me wisely choose what's right.

Day and Night Stick Puppets

Solomon Prays to Know What Is Right

1 Kings 3–4

These creative stick puppets add excitement to the Bible song "By My Helper."

Supplies

- the Bible song "Be My Helper" (p. 67)
- orange card stock (1 sheet)
- yellow card stock (1 sheet)
- 2 wiggle eyes
- 2 woode, craft sticks
- double-sided tape

Directions

Before class cut a large sun from the orange sheet of card stock. Cut a crescent-shape moon from the yellow sheet of card stock. Patterns are included on page 216. Glue a craft stick to the backs of the sun and moon as a handle for each. Tape two wiggle eyes to the front of the sun.

During class sing the Bible song "Be My Helper." When you sing the phrase "all day long," hold up the sun puppet. Continue to hold up the sun puppet as you sing the song. When you sing the phrase "day and night," hold up the moon puppet next to the sun. Continue to hold up both stick puppets as you sing. When you sing the phrase "wisely choose what's right," turn the crescent moon on its side and place it in front of the sun to make it smile. (See the illustrations below.)

Talk with children about the need to make good choices all the time. Remind the children that making good choices pleases God.

Activity Option

Consider making a pattern for the sun and the crescent moon from cardboard. Allow the children to trace and cut out their own sun and moon puppets. If you do this, consider simplifying the sun shape to a simple circle. Provide two craft sticks per child and tape so that kids can attach their puppets to the craft sticks. Provide wiggle eyes for the sun puppets (two per child) or allow children to draw eyes on the sun using crayons or washable markers. Children can sing the song using their own puppets or take them home and use their puppets as they sing the song for friends and family.

Come with Me to Build the Temple

Solomon Builds the Temple
1 Kings 5–8

Tune: "This Is the Way"

Come with me to build the temple,
build the temple, build the temple.
Come with me to build the temple,
a place to worship God.

We will go to sing and pray,
sing and pray, sing and pray.
We will go to sing and pray,
pray and worship God.

Block Play

Solomon Builds the Temple

1 Kings 5–8

Supplies

- "Come with Me to Build the Temple" Bible song (p. 70)
- building blocks

Directions

Teach the children the Bible song "Come with Me to Build the Temple." As you sing the song, allow the children to pretend to build the temple using building blocks.

Talk with the children about why it was important for King Solomon to build the temple. Talk about what hard work it is to build a building.

Close with prayer, thanking God for the people who work hard to build church buildings where people can go and worship God.

There's a Raven!

Elijah Is Fed by Ravens
1 Kings 17

Tune: "Frere Jacques"

Elijah's hungry, Elijah's hungry,
what to do? What to do?
God knows what he needs. God knows what he needs.
He'll send food. He'll send food.

There's a raven, there's a raven,
bringing bread, bringing meat.
Morning and night, morning and night,
food to eat, food to eat.

When I'm hungry, when I'm hungry,
what to do? What to do?
God know what I need. God knows what I need.
He gives food. He gives food.

Feathers and Bread Raven

Elijah Is Fed by Ravens
1 Kings 17

Supplies

- copies of the Feathers and Bread Raven pattern (p. 211) printed on white card stock
- black and yellow crayons or washable markers
- black craft feathers
- glue
- oyster crackers

Directions

Give each child a picture of a raven. Direct the children to color the raven black and its beak and claws yellow. Help children glue black craft feathers to the bird's body. Glue an oyster cracker to the bird's beak as a reminder that the ravens brought food to Elijah.

Talk with the children about how God cared for Elijah and gave him food. Tell the children that we can trust God to give us what we need.

Close with prayer, thanking God for knowing what we need and for taking good care of us.

Elijah and the Widow

Elijah Helps a Widow
1 Kings 17

Elijah asked a widow for

some water and some bread.
(pretend to eat and drink)

"My son and I have just enough for one more meal," she said.
(hold up one finger)

"If you will share your meal with me,
(point out; point to self)

God will give you what you need."
(nod head yes)

The widow shared, a meal prepared,
(hold out hands as though sharing)

God surely fed all three.
(hold up three fingers, nod yes)

Obey Poster

Elijah Helps a Widow
1 Kings 17

Make these posters as reminders that the widow was blessed when she obeyed God.

Supplies

- 11" x 17" paper, card stock, or poster board (1 per child)
- black permanent marker
- food pictures cut from magazines or grocery ads
- small, white paper plates (1 per child)
- various stickers of food items
- glue sticks
- crayons or washable markers

Directions

Before class cut several pictures of food from magazines or grocery ads. Cut enough so each child can have three to five pictures each. Print the letters *bey* on each sheet of 11" x 17" paper. Leave space on the left for children to attach paper plates later.

During give each child a paper plate and allow them to choose a few pictures of food. Assist children in gluing the food pictures to their plates. Children can color the rims of the paper plates using crayons or washable markers.

Give each child a sheet of 11" x 17" paper, card stock, or poster board with the letters bey pre-printed. Children should attach their paper plates to their posters so that the paper plate forms the letter O in the word *obey*.

Children can finish decorating their posters using stickers of various food items placed randomly around the poster.

Talk with children about how the widow obeyed God by sharing her food with Elijah. Elijah also obeyed God by helping the widow and her son with the food they needed.

The Widow and Her Son

Elijah Helps a Widow's Son
1 Kings 17

A widow had a son who was sick and then he died.
(cross hands over stomach)

The widow was so sad that she cried, and cried, and cried.
(point to checks)

Elijah was a man of God and a man of prayer.
(place hands together as though praying)

"Give the boy to me," he said, and then he climbed the stairs.
(walk fingers upstairs)

Elijah gently laid the boy down upon his bed.
(lay hand in flat palm of other hand

A very simple prayer Elijah knelt and said.
(place hands together as though praying)

"O Lord, my God," he said, "let this boy live again."

And then the boy began breathing out and breathing in!
(breathe deeply in and out)

"See, your son lives!" The widow answered, "Yes, it's true!"
(smile)

"I know you are a man from God and that He speaks through you."
(point up and then out)

Prayer Chain

Elijah Helps a Widow's Son
1 Kings 17

Supplies

- colored construction paper
- scissors
- black permanent marker
- tape

Directions

Before class cut several sheets of construction paper into 1" x 12" strips.

During class talk with the children about prayer. Remind the children that God always listens to our prayers. Ask the children to name someone or something they would like to pray about. As the children give their ideas, write their responses on the strips of paper.

Help the children make a Prayer Chain by looping the strips and taping them at the ends. Assemble the chain by interlocking each link as you go.

Hang the chain in the classroom as a reminder that God always listens when we pray.

Contest on Mount Carmel

Elijah and the Prophets of Baal
1 Kings 18

Tune: "Froggie Went a-Courtin'"

There was a contest on Mount Carmel. Oh yes!
There was a contest on Mount Carmel. Oh yes!
Elijah and some other men
came to see who God would send
some fire from the sky to prove them right. Oh yes!

The prophets of Baal prayed and shouted out. Oh yes!
The prophets of Baal prayed and shouted out. Oh yes!
The prophets of Baal shouted out.
Then they jumped around and danced about.
But Baal did not send fire from the sky. Oh no!

Elijah built an altar to the Lord. Oh yes!
Elijah built an altar to the Lord. Oh yes!
He placed some meat up on the wood,
took some water—soaked it good.
His God would send down fire from the sky. Oh yes!

Elijah offered up a simple prayer. Oh yes!
Elijah offered up a simple prayer. Oh yes!
Elijah asked for fire to fall.
Then down came a fireball.
God showed that He's the one true God of all. Oh yes!

Fireball Toss

Elijah and the Prophets of Baal

1 Kings 18

This activity will help children visualize the fire sent from heaven as they play games by tossing their own fireball.

Supplies

- red, orange, and yellow yarn
- cardboard (8” long and 4” wide)
- scissors
- large basket

Directions

Before class make several fireballs from the three colors of yarn.

Step 1: Hold the ends of all three colors of yarn at the edge of the cardboard and begin wrapping the yarn lengthwise around the cardboard. Repeat this as many times as desired; the more times the yarn is wrapped around the cardboard, the fuller the fireballs will be.

Step 2: When you are finished wrapping, carefully slide the yarn off of the cardboard and tightly tie the yarn at the center with a separate piece of yarn.

Step 3: Once the loops are tied at the center, cut the loops apart at both ends to make the fireball.

Step 4: The fireball is complete! Make as many as you like for the number of children in your class.

During class allow the children to toss the fireballs to one another or try tossing them into a large basket. This activity will help children visualize the fire sent from heaven as they play games by tossing their own fireballs.

Activity Option

Allow children to make their own fireballs in class. An adult will need to help with tying the fireballs at the center. Supervise the children as they cut the yarn loops apart at each end. Children can take their fireballs home as a reminder of the day’s lesson.

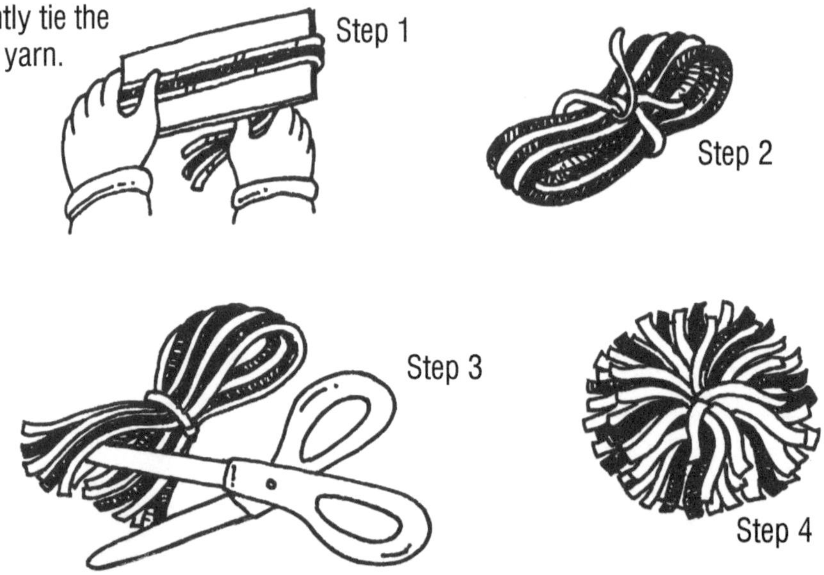

Elisha and the Widow

Elisha and a Widow's Oil
2 Kings 4

A widow had a problem but she knew just what to do.
(point to your temple; nod head yes)

She went to see Elisha—God's prophet kind and true.
(place hand over eyes as though searching; place hand over heart)

He had a plan to help her. In fact he helped a lot.
(point to your temple; nod head yes)

He told her to pour cooking oil into many pots.
(pretend to pour)

When all the pots were filled up, the oil came to a stop.
(put hand up to stop)

No more oil would flow out, not even one more drop.
(shake head no; hold up one finger)

And then the boy began breathing out and breathing in!
(breathe deeply in and out)

We can be like Elisha, helping every day.
(nod head yes; motion outward)

To find a way to help another, listen, watch and pray.
(point to ear; point to eye; fold hands in prayer)

Pots and Pans Water Play

Elisha and a Widow's Oil
2 Kings 4

Supplies

- water table or large tub filled with water
- oversize shirts to use as smocks
- small metal pots and pans
- dishtowels

Directions

Young children love water play! Give each child an oversize shirt to protect her clothing. Allow children to play with the pots and pans in the water play area.

As children fill pots to overflowing, talk about the widow's pots that were miraculously filled with oil. When it is time to clean up, ask the children to practice being good helpers. Children can use dishtowels to dry the pots and pans

Shunammite Woman

Elisha and a Shunammite Family
2 Kings 4

Tune: "Make New Friends"

The Shunammite woman was kind and sharing.
The Shunammite woman was very kind.

She built a room for Elisha.
She built a room for Elisha.

Who is kind? Who is sharing?
I can be kind and sharing too.

Sharing Hands

Elisha and a Shunammite Family
2 Kings 4

These Sharing Hands will help children think about how they can look for ways to share with others.

Supplies

- "Shunammite Woman" Bible song (p. 81)
- copy of the Sharing Hands pattern for each child (p. 212)
- large metal coffee can with a plastic lid
- colored copy paper
- dpuble-sided tape
- black permanent marker
- various pictures of eyes cut from magazines or found on the Internet
- scissors
- crayons or washable markers

Directions

Before class prepare a Sharing Hands can. Begin by wrapping copy paper of any color around a coffee can and securing it with tape. You may need to trim the paper to fit exactly, depending on the size of the can you are using. Write "I Can Share" on the covered can. Decorate the can with pictures of eyes that you have cut from magazines or have found on the Internet.

Cut a slit in the plastic lid long enough to slide the Sharing Hands into the can. The hands can be folded in half to fit through the slit if necessary.

During class help children cut out the hands around the solid outline. Ask the children to name one thing they can share with someone. Help children write what they can share. Allow younger children who cannot write to draw a picture of what they can share on their Sharing Hands. Use crayons or washable markers. Make sure that the children's names are also written somewhere on the hands.

Teach the children the Bible song "Shunammite Woman." As you sing, invite the children to drop their Sharing Hands into the can.

Explain to the children that the can is decorated with eyes because the Shunammite woman saw a need that Elisha had and shared something of her own with him. We should also look for ways we can share with others.

God Has Power

Elisha and the Shunammite's Son
2 Kings 4

Tune: "Happy Birthday"

Mighty God has power.
Mighty God has power.
Mighty God has all power to help you and me.

Mighty God healed the sick.
Mighty God raised the dead.
Mighty God has all power to help you and me.

Power Movement

Elisha and the Shunammite's Son

2 Kings 4

Supplies

- "God Has Power" Bible song (p. 83)

Directions

Teach the children the Bible song "God Has Power." Every time you sing the word *power*, lead the children in making a strength motion by flexing their arm muscles. Each time you sing the word *sick*, lead the children in clutching their stomachs as though they're not feeling well. When you sing the word *dead*, lead the children in tilting their heads to one side and closing their eyes. Repeat these motions each time you sing the song.

Once the children have learned the motions, select volunteers to come to the front of the room and lead the motions themselves.

Naaman Was Sick and Then Healed

Elisha and Naaman
2 Kings 5

Tune: "Skip to My Lou"

Naaman was sick. What did he do?
Naaman was sick. What did he do?
Naaman was sick. What did he do?
He went to see Elisha!

Elisha told Naaman, "Wash in the Jordan."
Elisha told Naaman, "Wash in the Jordan."
Elisha told Naaman, "Wash in the Jordan."
"Wash seven times in the Jordan."

Chorus
Dip, dip, dip, Naaman you.
Dip, dip, dip, Naaman you.
Dip, dip, dip, Naaman you.
Dip seven times in the Jordan.

Naaman washed in the Jordan and was healed.
Naaman washed in the Jordan and was healed.
Naaman washed in the Jordan and was healed.
He went to see Elisha!

Now I know there is no other God.
Now I know there is no other God.
Now I know there is no other God,
none but the God of heaven.

Repeat chorus

Thumb Up for Naaman

Elisha and Naaman
2 Kings 5

Supplies

- "Naaman Was Sick and Then Healed" Bible song (p. 86)

Directions

Teach the children the Bible song "Naaman Was Sick and Then Healed." Each time you say the word *dip*, have the children make a motion with their thumbs. Start with the thumb up. Turn the wrist to one side, bring the thumb down and back up, as though dipping.

As a class make up motions for the remaining parts of the song. Some suggestions would be to shrug your shoulders when you sing the phrase "What did he do?" or pretend to wash as though taking a bath when you sing the phrase "Wash in the Jordan."

Remind the children that God is powerful and that He healed Naaman. Close with prayer, thanking God for being such a great and powerful God.

King Josiah

Josiah Reads God's Word
2 Kings 22–23

Tune: "Old King Cole"

King Josiah was a faithful young king,
and a faithful young king was he.
He called for repairs to the Lord's temple church,
and for the temple money.

While the repairs were being made,
something important was found.
The Book of Teachings—the Lord's holy Word—
was found just lying around.

King Josiah was very upset.
He wept and he tore his clothes.
God's holy Word must be read to all
so everyone will know.

Pound and Found

Josiah Reads God's Word

2 Kings 22–23

Supplies

- "King Josiah" Bible song (p. 87)
- toy hammers
- small wooden blocks
- small Bible or paper scroll

Directions

Teach the children the Bible song "King Josiah." Help the children strike toy hammers against wooden blocks with the beat of the song.

After singing the song, have one child hide the Bible or scroll somewhere around the room while the other children close their eyes. After the Bible or scroll is hidden, have the children search for it until it is found.

Talk with the children about how important God's Word is and about how sad it would be if it were really lost.

Close with prayer, thanking God for giving us His Word.

Jehoshaphat

Jehoshaphat Asks for God's Help

2 Chronicles 17, 20

Jehoshaphat was Judah's king.
(place pretend crown on head)

He loved the Lord more than anything.
(cross arms over chest)

He worshipped God and he would pray
(point up; place hands together as though praying)

when he needed help—night or day.
(tilt head and fold hands by face as though sleeping; head up as though awake)

God heard his prayers and helped him out.
(cup hands at ear as though listening)

People praised with songs and shouts.
(cup hands at mouth as though shouting)

And then the boy began breathing out and breathing in!
(breathe deeply in and out)

We can pray for this and that
(point to self)

and ask for help like Jehoshaphat.
(place hands together as though praying)

Prayer Picture

Jehoshaphat Asks for God's Help
2 Chronicles 17, 20

Supplies
- copies of the Prayer Picture pattern (p. 213)
- crayons or washable markers

Directions
Give each child a copy of the Prayer Picture. Ask the children to think of one thing they would like to pray about. Once every child has thought of something, help him illustrate his prayer on the praying hands. For younger children who may have trouble with this, you may need to write the request on the praying hands for them instead.

Talk with the children about how God hears all of our prayers. When each child has completed his Prayer Picture, pray as a class for each request.

Activity Option
Create a prayer tree in your classroom. Make a trunk and some branches from brown roll paper or brown grocery bags and attach the tree to a wall using reusable adhesive. Attach the praying hands like leaves on each branch of the tree. As each prayer is answered, take that hand off of the tree and attach it near the base of the trunk (like leaves that have fallen). Over time you and the children in your class will be able to see all of the prayers that God has answered.

Nehemiah

Nehemiah Rebuilds the Wall
Nehemiah 1–2, 4, 6

Tune: "Mary Had a Little Lamb"

Nehemiah heard God's call,
"Go rebuild the city wall."
Rock by rock, it was built tall
with help from one and all.

Then he called to one and all,
"Must rebuild the city wall."
Rock by rock, it was built tall,
so strong it did not fall.

Sing and Stack

Nehemiah Rebuilds the Wall
Nehemiah 1–2, 4, 6

Supplies

- "Nehemiah" Bible song (p. 92)
- building blocks or boxes for stacking

Directions

Teach the children the Bible song "Nehemiah." As they sing the song, allow the children to pretend to build the wall like Nehemiah did. Repeat the song, but this time, sing the song in a key that is a half step higher as you continue to build the wall. Raise the key each time you repeat the song and add to the wall as you sing. As the song gets higher, so will your wall!

Brave Esther

Esther Helps God's People
Esther 2–5, 8

The king was looking for a wife—the prettiest he could find.
(place hand over eyes as though searching)

Esther was the one he chose, but trouble was not far behind.
(shake head no)

Esther had a secret, for she was born a Jew.
(put finger to lips as though being quiet)

Some people did not like them—no one in the palace knew.
(shake head no; point to side of head)

Esther made a choice to help her people out.
(extend hand)

She had to have a plan, so she hurried all about.
(point to side of head)

Brave Esther went into her room,
(let fingers look as though they are walking)

three days to fast and pray.
(hold up three fingers; fold hands in prayer)

When ready she went to the king
(bow)

the Jews were saved that day.
(place arms up as though celebrating)

Esther Crowns

Esther Helps God's People

Esther 2–5, 8

Supplies

- "Brave Esther" action rhyme (p. 93)
- copies of the crown (p. 211)
- colored copy paper
- crayons or washable markers
- scissors
- adhesive jewels (1 per child)
- tape

Directions

Before class cut several strips of colored copy paper that are 1" x 12" each.

During class give each child a crown to color. Help the children cut out the crowns.

Give each child an adhesive jewel to attach to the crown. Tape a strip of construction paper to one side of each crown. Size each crown to fit each child's head and tape the other end of the paper strip to the opposite side of the crown. This will form the headband for the crown.

Kids can wear their crowns as they act out the "Brave Esther" action rhyme.

Daniel and His Friends

Daniel and His Friends Obey God

Daniel 1

Daniel and his three good friends,
(hold up one finger; hold up four fingers)

were not afraid of other men.
(shake head no)

They always chose to do what was right.
(nod head yes)

They were good men in God's sight.
(point up)

They did not want to seem so rude
(shake head no)

but only ate the healthy food.
(pretend to eat)

They were picked to serve the king.
(pretend to place crown on head)

They chose the right in everything.
(nod head yes)

Just like them we can obey
(point to self)

and make good choices every day.
(nod head yes)

Honor God in every way,
(point up)

by what we do and what we say.
(place arms out; point to mouth)

Obey Place Mats

Daniel and His Friends Obey God
Daniel 1

Supplies
- 11" x 17" card stock
- black permanent marker
- pictures of vegetables cut from magazines or printed from the Internet
- glue sticks
- various vegetable stickers
- crayons or washable markers
- clear adhesive covering

Directions
Before class print the words "We Can Obey God" in the center of each piece of card stock.

During class allow each child to decorate his or her paper using pictures of vegetables cut from magazines or taken from the Internet, various vegetable stickers, and crayons or washable markers. When the children are finished decorating their paper, cover each sheet using clear contact paper or laminate the place mats if possible

Allow children to take their place mats home as a reminder that just like Daniel and his friends obeyed God, we can obey God too!

Shadrach, Meshach, Abednego

Daniel's Friends Worship Only God
Daniel 3

Tune: "John Jacob Jingleheimer Schmidt"

Shadrach, Meshach, Abednego,
these three would not bow down
to idols made of gold,
and soon the king was told.
Into the furnace they were thrown!
Hot! Hot! Hot! Hot! Hot! Hot!
Hot!

Shadrach, Meshach, Abednego
chose to do what was right.
And when the king looked in,
he saw four, not three men,
walking around and burning not!
Not! Not! Not! Not! Not! Not!
Not!

Shadrach, Meshach, Abednego—
I want to be like them.
Obeying God above
and trusting in His love,
living each day to honor Him,
yes, yes, yes, yes,
I'll honor Him.

Take a Stand

Daniel's Friends Worship Only God
Daniel 3

Supplies

- "Shadrach, Meshach, Abednego" Bible song (p. 97)

Directions

Teach the children the Bible song "Shadrach, Meshach, Abednego." After the children have learned the song and can follow along with the words, divide them into three groups.

The first group is the Shadrach group. They should sing hot seven times at the end of the first verse. The second group is the Meshach group. They should sing not seven times at the end of the second verse. The third group is the Abednego group. They should sing yes four times and then have everyone sing "I'll honor Him" phrase at the end of the third verse of the song.

Practice the song with each group standing when they are to sing their words. You may need to practice a few times so the children become comfortable with their parts.

Writing on the Wall

Daniel and the Handwriting on the Wall
Daniel 5

Handwriting on the wall—what does it mean?
(pretend to write in air)

It means the king has done a very bad thing.
(shake finger as though scolding; shake head no)

He drank from golden cups and worshipped statues made by man.
(pretend to drink and hammer)

He did not honor God or follow God's plan.
(shake head no)

Daniel told the truth, though it was hard to do.
(point to mouth)

He spoke the words of God, and then it all came true.
(point up; nod head yes)

Do the right thing, love God and obey.
(nod head yes; point up)

Show your love to Him, by what you do and say.
(cross arms over chest; arms out; point to mouth)

Wall Writing

Daniel and the Handwriting on the Wall

Daniel 5

Supplies

- roll paper
- reusable adhesive
- crayons or washable markers

Directions

Kids love to write on walls! With this activity they'll finally get their chance! Attach two long sheets of roll paper to a wall in the room. Attach them low enough so kids can reach the entire area of the paper. Make sure that the entire wall surface within reach of the children is covered by paper.

During class talk with the children about the handwriting that appeared on the wall in Daniel 5. Allow kids to write on the paper you've prepared as you talk about what the king might have thought when he saw a hand on the wall writing words that he didn't understand.

Activity Option

For older children, you can turn this in to a game of charades! Since in the story what appeared on the wall had to be discerned by Daniel, allow the children to draw images on the paper while the class guesses what is being drawn.

Daniel

Daniel and the Lions' Den
Daniel 6

Handwriting on the wall—what does it mean?
(point up; place hands on head like a crown)

A wise and faithful servant, he did his best in everything.
(point to temple on side of head; arms out)

But jealous, mean people tricked the king to make a rule.
(pretend to write on palm)

"No worship, prayers, or songs to God!" announced the king, now fooled.
(place hands together as though praying; cup hands at mouth)

But at the open window, Daniel dared to pray and sit.
(draw square in the air with fingers; place hands together as though praying)

So soldiers of the mighty king tossed Daniel in a pit.
(make muscles with arms; point down)

The lions did not eat him—not one tiny, little bite.
(shake head no)

God kept Daniel safe and sound throughout the long dark night.
(nod head yes)

And when the sun came up and they looked into the ground,
(place hand over eyes as though searching; look up first and then down)

Daniel praying to the Lord, is what the people found.
(place hands together as though praying)

There is no other mighty God, so powerful and true.
(make muscles with arms)

Thank you faithful Daniel, I learned these things from you.
(point out)

3-D Praying Hands

Daniel and the Lions' Den
Daniel 6

These fun 3-D pictures will remind kinds that we can pray to God just like Daniel did.

Supplies

- copies of the Prayer Picture (p. 213)
- card stock
- black permanent marker
- scissors
- crayons in various skin tones
- cotton balls
- glue

Directions

Before class lay the card stock in the horizontal position and print the words "We Can Pray to God" at the top of each paper.

During class give each child a copy of the Prayer Picture. Allow children to color their praying hands using crayons in various skin tones. Assist children in cutting out the praying hands on the solid line.

When children are finished coloring and cutting, give each child several cotton balls and some glue. Help children glue the cotton balls to the center of the card stock in a tight bunch. Once the cotton balls are glued in place, assist children in dotting glue on top of the cotton balls.

Place the praying hands over the cotton balls and press down onto the paper. The cotton balls underneath will make the praying hands pop up, giving them a 3-D effect.

Read the words at the top of the page to the children. Remind them that we can pray to God just like Daniel did. Talk with children about how Daniel trusted God to help him. We can trust that God will hear and answer our prayers too.

Oh, Jonah

Jonah Tells about God
Jonah 1–3:

Tune: "Skip to My Lou"

God told Jonah preach in Nineveh.
God told Jonah preach in Nineveh.
God told Jonah preach in Nineveh.
Go and preach in Nineveh.

Chorus
Oh, Jonah, go preach in Nineveh.
Oh, Jonah, go preach in Nineveh.
Oh, Jonah, go preach in Nineveh.
Go and preach in Nineveh.

To run away from God, Jonah set sail.
A storm blew in, and winds began to wail.
To run away from God, Jonah set sail.
Jonah ran away from God.

Repeat chorus

Jonah said to them, "Throw me in the sea.
I disobeyed God, and He's angry with me."
Jonah said to them, "Throw me in the sea."
And they threw him in the sea.

Repeat chorus

Swallowed by a fish three nights and days.
Jonah turned to God, and then he prayed.
Swallowed by a fish three nights and days.
Finally Jonah prayed.

Repeat chorus

The fish spat Jonah onto dry land.
Jonah decided to follow God's plan.
The fish spat Jonah onto dry land.
Jonah followed God.

Repeat chorus

Paper Bag Whale

Jonah Tells about God

Jonah 1–3:

These puffy whales make great reminders that we should tell others about God just as Jonah learned.

Supplies

- brown paper bags in any size
- crayons or washable markers
- large adhesive wiggle eyes *(optional)*
- several old newspapers or tissue paper to use as stuffing
- rubber bands
- scissors

Directions

With the brown paper bags folded flat, help the children draw mouths on the bottoms of the paper bags and color the mouths red. Using a black marker, write the words “God helps us to tell about Him” on the bottom of each bag. The first part of the sentence should be written above the mouth, the word tell should be written inside the mouth, and the last two words should be written below the mouth (see illustration).

Have the children open the bags. Assist the children in attaching the wiggle eyes to the sides of the bag whale. If you have chosen not to use wiggle eyes, allow the children to draw the eyes using crayons or washable markers.

On the front of the bag, have children draw a a dark circle for the blowhole.

Using old newspapers, help children stuff their whales until the bags are two-thirds full. Help the children wrap a rubber band around the unstuffed portion of the bag to make a tail. Fan out the tail and trim with scissors as necessary.

Children can use their paper bag whales as a reminder of the story of Jonah and that it is important to tell others about God.

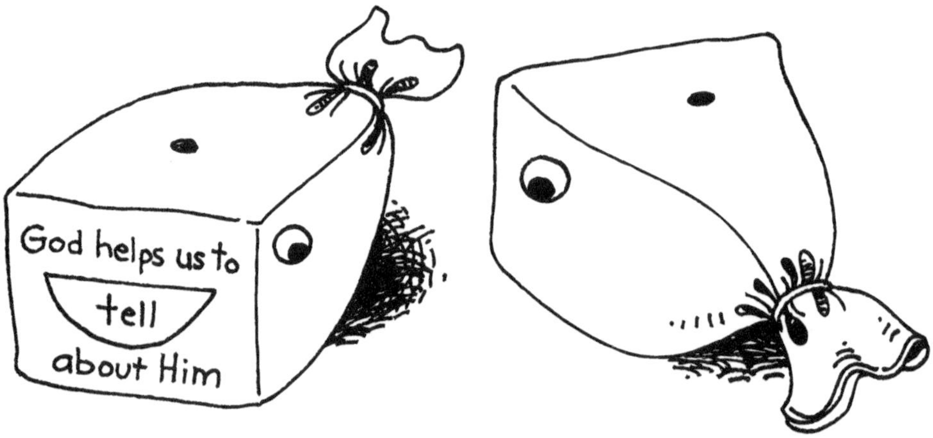

Angel Greetings

An Angel Announces Jesus' Birth;
An Angel Brings Special News
Matthew 1; Luke 1

An angel came to Mary with greetings of great joy.
(open arms wide)

Smile and be happy. You'll have a baby boy.
(smile and hold arms as though rocking a baby)

His name will be Jesus, sent from God above.
(point up)

Smile and be happy. He'll show us God's great love.
(cross arms over chest)

Good News Angel Ornaments

An Angel Announces Jesus' Birth; An Angel Brings Special News
Matthew 1; Luke 1

Supplies

- white coffee filters (2 per child)
- medium-sized lollipops (1 per child)
- thin ribbon in any color
- sparkling chenille wire (2" piece per child)
- hot glue gun and glue sticks
- washable and glitter markers
- wire ornament hooks
- scissors

Directions

Before class prepare one angel ornament for each child to decorate. Fold one coffee filter into fourths and tape the center point to the top of the ball of a medium-sized lollipop. Place another coffee filter over the lollipop and secure it with a ribbon tied in a bow (see the illustration below). Cut a sparkling chenille wire into 2" pieces. Bend them into the shape of a circle to make a halo and glue it on the top of the lollipop using a hot glue gun.

During class help the children draw happy faces on their angels, using washable markers. Assist children in decorating the bottom edges of the coffee filter using glitter markers.

Finally, add the ornament hooks by hooking the small loop through the ribbon at the back of th angel's head.

Encourage children to give their ornaments away as they tell others about the angel delivering special news that Jesus was to be born.

Greeting Card Birth Announcement

An Angel Announces Jesus' Birth;
An Angel Brings Special News
Matthew 1; Luke 1

Supplies

- card stock in any color (1 per child)
- black permanent marker
- scissors
- images from the Internet or scraps of wrapping paper that tell about Jesus' birth
- glue, glue sticks, or double-sided tape
- crayons or washable markers
- angel stickers or other nativity stickers

Directions

Before class, fold one sheet of card stock in half for each child. Inside the card write "Jesus Is Born."

During class help children cut out scenes from the Internet or scraps of wrapping paper telling about Jesus' birth. Tape or glue the scenes to the fronts of their cards. Assist children in signing their names inside their cards. Children can decorate the insides of their cards using angel stickers or other nativity stickers.

Encourage children to give their announcement cards to friends and tell about how an angel announced that Jesus would be born.

Oh, It's Jesus

Jesus Is Born; A Special Baby Is Born
Luke 1–2

Tune: "Little Liza Jane"

Who's that wrapped in strips of cloth
there on the hay?

We celebrate Jesus' birth
this special day.

Chorus
Oh, it's Jesus, God's only Son.
Oh, it's Jesus rejoice; He's come!

Mary, Joseph, animals,
there at His birth.

Angels told the shepherds and
sang peace on earth.

Repeat chorus

Anna and old Simeon
thought "Could it be?"
Baby Jesus, God's own Son—
a sight to see!

Repeat chorus

Dramatic Play

Jesus Is Born; A Special Baby Is Born

Luke 1–2

Supplies

- "Oh, It's Jesus" Bible song (p. 108)
- boxes
- hay or yellow Easter grass
- dolls
- strips of muslin cloth

Directions

Before class, create a dramatic play center where children can pretend to be Mary, Joseph, angels, and shepherds on the night Jesus was born. Place hay or yellow Easter grass inside several boxes and place the boxes the play center. These can be used as mangers. Place several dolls and strips of cloth in the play center as well.

When children arrive, show them how to swaddle or wrap the dolls.

Allow children to take turns playing in the center as you sing the Bible song "Oh, It's Jesus."

Star Chain

Jesus Is Born; A Special Baby Is Born

Luke 1–2

These chains spell out Jesus' name and are fun decorations for kids to use at home or in the classroom.

Supplies

- copy of the star pattern found for each (p. 214)
- yellow card stock *(optional)*
- scissors
- 5 strips of yellow construction paper (1" x 9") per child
- washable markers
- 4 strips of white construction paper (1" x 9") per child
- tape

Directions

Before class copy and cut out one star for each child from pattern. Copy the pattern onto yellow card stock or allow children to color the stars yellow in class. Cut a slit in each star where indicated by the horizontal line.

During class give each child five yellow strips of construction paper. Assist children in laying the strips vertically in front of themselves and writing one letter of Jesus' name on each strip (see illustration). Help children slide the yellow strip with the letter J through the slit in the star so that the J is showing. Attach the strip so that it forms the first loop in the chain. Continue with the activity, alternating white and yellow strips until the chain is completed and the name Jesus is spelled out completely.

Use the chains to decorate the classroom or allow children to take their chains home.

Discuss with the children that Jesus was a special baby and we are happy that He was born.

Option for Younger Children

Omit writing the letters of Jesus' name and simply have them alternate yellow and white strips to make their chains.

Hurry Shepherds

Shepherds Hear Special News;
Shepherds Visit Jesus
Luke 2

Tune: "Baa, Baa, Black Sheep"

Hurry, shepherds quickly, quickly run,
to the stable; see God's Son!
Look, He's asleep in a manger bed,
wrapped in cloth like the angels said.
Hurry, shepherds, quickly, quickly run,
to the stable; see God's Son!

Candy Cane Message

Shepherds Visit Jesus; Shepherds Hear Special News

Luke 2

Supplies

- copy of the Candy Cane Message pattern (p. 215; 1 per child)
- white card stock
- crayons or washable markers
- small candy canes (1 per child)
- tape

Directions

Print copies of the Candy Cane Message pattern on white card sctock. Help children color the letters on the Candy Cane Message.

Explain to children that the candy cane looks like a shepherd's staff when it is turned one direction. When it is turned the other direction, it looks like the letter J, the first letter of Jesus' name.

Assist children in taping their candy canes to their pages to form a J at the beginning of Jesus' name.

Encourage children to give their paper messages to others as they tell about the shepherds hearing the special news that Jesus was born.

Go and Tell

Shepherds Visit Jesus; Shepherds Hear Special New
Luke 2

Supplies

- doll wrapped in cloth
- box
- masking tape

Directions

Play this relay game with the children in your class as a reminder that the shepherds were the first to hear the news of Jesus' birth and were also the first to visit the special baby.

Place a doll in a box on one side of the classroom. The doll represents baby Jesus. On the opposite side of the room, have the children line up single file behind a line of masking tape. The children represent shepherds.

When the teacher gives the signal, the first child, or "shepherd" should run to "baby Jesus" and circle the "manger." The child should then run back to the next "shepherd" in line and say to him or her, "Jesus is born!" After hearing these words, that "shepherd" should repeat the actions of the first, and so on, until everyone has had a chance to travel to see "Jesus" and tell the good news to others.

Anna and Simeon

Simeon and Anna See Jesus

Luke 2

Tune: "Rock-a-Bye Baby"

Anna and Simeon were very old.
But Simeon would see Jesus, he was told.

There in the temple they worshiped and prayed.

And for baby Jesus they waited each day.

Mary and Joseph brought the baby boy.
Anna and Simeon were filled with joy.
There in the temple they thanked God above.

He sent us His Son and He showed us His love.

Act It Out!

Simeon and Anna See Jesus
Luke 2

Supplies

- "Anna and Simeon" Bible song (p. 114)
- girl to play the part of Anna
- boy to play the part of Simeon
- props to make Anna and Simeon appear elderly (shawl, cane, glasses, sweater, etc.)
- doll
- girl to play the part of Mary
- boy to play the part of Joseph

Directions

Teach the children the Bible song "Anna and Simeon." Choose one girl and one boy to play the parts of Anna and Simeon and one girl and one boy to play the parts of Mary and Joseph. Give the children playing Mary and Joseph the doll. Give the props to the two children playing Anna and Simeon and show them how to use the props to make themselves appear elderly.

Sing the Bible song a few times. Once children are familiar with the words, allow the children you've chosen to act out the words in the song.

Sing the song several times, choosing new children each time to play the parts. Trade the props as new children are chosen to play the parts of Anna and Simeon.

Discuss with the children why we are thankful Jesus was born.

Close with prayer, thanking God for sending His Son into the world.

Weary Wise Men

Wise Men Worship Jesus;
Wise Men Worship a Special Baby
Matthew 2

Weary wise men traveled far,
(place hand over eyes as though searching)

led by the light of a special star.
(point to sky)

To worship Jesus as the king,
(bow head; fold hands as though praying)

precious gifts to Him they bring.
(stretch arms forward)

I do not have to travel far
(shake head no)

or see the light of a special star.
(point up; shake head no)

I can worship Him as king,
(bow head; fold hands as though praying)

my heart and life to Him I bring.
(place hand over heart; reach arms up)

Worship from Our Hearts

Wise Men Worship Jesus
Wise Men Worship a Special Baby
Matthew 2

Supplies

- empty box wrapped as a birthday gift with a bow and a tag reading "To Jesus"
- 2 white paper hearts for each child
- washable markers

Directions

Before class make a slit in the top of the gift box large enough for the hearts to slide through.

During class talk with the children about ways they can worship Jesus like the wise men did. Point out that the wise men brought thoughtful gifts and gave them freely from their hearts.

Ask children to draw pictures on their hearts of themselves giving gifts to Jesus. If the children need gift ideas, talk about how singing, praying, bringing friends to church, giving money, and helping others are all ways of giving to Jesus.

Lead the Children in the "Weary Wise Men" rhyme (p. 116). As you say the rhyme, let the children place the hearts they have made into the gift box.

Close with prayer, thanking God for sending Jesus into the world.

Wise Men Worship

Wise Men Worship Jesus; Wise Men Worship a Special Baby

Matthew 2

Tune: "Twinkle, Twinkle, Little Star"

Weary wise men traveled far,
led by the light of a special star.
To worship Jesus as the king,
precious gifts to Him they bring.
Weary wise men traveled far,
led by the light of a special star.

I don't have to travel far
or see the light of a special star.
I can worship Him as king.
My heart and life to Him I bring.
You don't have to travel far.
You can worship where you are.

Star Sticks

Wise Men Worship Jesus
Wise Men Worship a Special Baby
Matthew 2

Children will enjoy making these sparkling Star Sticks and using them as they sing about the wise men following a star as they traveled to worship Jesus.

Supplies

- "Wise Men Worship" Bible song (p. 118)
- copy of the small stars (p. 214; 1 per child)
- card stock
- scissors
- crayons or washable markers
- craft sticks (1 per child)
- glitter markers
- glue

Directions

Copy the small stars onto white card stock. Cut them out and give two stars to each child. During class children can color their stars yellow. Help children decorate their stars using glitter markers. Apply the glitter around the edges of each star. Allow the stars to dry for 20 to 30 minutes.

Once the stars are dry, attach the stars to craft sticks by gluing one star to each side of the stick.

Children can wave their star sticks as they sing the Bible song "Wise Men Worship."

Boy Jesus in the Temple

Jesus as a Boy
Luke 2

Tune: "Eensy Weensy Spider"

Jesus and His parents took a trip one day.
They went to the temple to worship and to pray.
When relatives and family started to go home,
Jesus stayed behind in the city on His own.

Mary and Joseph went searching all around;
there in the temple Jesus could be found.
Talking with the teachers and sharing in God's Word,
"This is where I had to be" is what His parents heard.

Jesus then went home with His parents on that day.
He always chose to listen and always to obey.
Jesus was good and kind and caring too.
Listen and obey what your parents say to do.

Looking for Jesus Scopes

Jesus as a Boy
Luke 2

Supplies

- paper towel tubes (1 per child)
- black permanent marker
- crayons or washable markers
- Jesus stickers (p. 217)
- various decorative embellishments (glitter markers, ribbon, etc.)

Directions

Before class, using a black marker, write "Looking for Jesus" on the side of each paper towel tube.

During class give each child a paper towel tube. Allow children to decorate their tubes using crayons or washable markers. Children can attach various Jesus stickers to the outsides of their tubes as a reminder that Jesus' parents went looking for Him at the temple. Allow children to decorate their tubes using other various embellishments that you've provided. Children can use their Looking Scopes and pretend to look for Jesus, just as Mary and Joseph did in Jerusalem.

Jesus Pleased God

Jesus Is Baptized
Matthew 3; Mark 1

Walking, walking, walking to the riverside one day.
(motion hands as though walking fingers on palm)

Jesus walked to be baptized—He walked a long, long way.
(motion hands as though walking fingers on palm)

John tried to stop Him because Jesus had no sin.
(hold hand up to stop)

But Jesus said to John, "I must do this, my friend."
(nod head yes)

Jesus saw God's Spirit coming like a white dove bird.
(wiggle fingers like a bird flapping wings)

And speaking out of heaven, the voice of God was heard.
(cup hand to ear)

Jesus always pleased God, and we can please God too
(smile and nod head yes)

when we choose to listen and to do what's right and true.
(cup hand to ear; smile and nod head yes)

John and Jesus Stick Puppets

Jesus Is Baptized
Matthew 3; Mark 1

These stick puppets help children reenact Jesus' baptism as the children explore ways they can please God.

Supplies

- large wooden craft sticks (2 per child)
- brown fine-tip permanent marker
- black fine-tip permanent marker
- a water table or large containers of water

Directions

Before class prepare the stick figures by drawing a face on one end of each craft stick. Draw one with a black marker (John) and one with a brown marker (Jesus). Add feet and hands to complete each stick figure (see illustration).

Give each child one Jesus figure and one John figure. Encourage the children to reenact the story of Jesus' baptism by dipping their stick puppets in the water. Talk about how Jesus pleased God and how we can please God.

No! Go Away!

Jesus Is Tempted
Matthew 4

Satan came to Jesus—No! Go away!
(shake head no; extend arm and point out)

Satan tried to trick Him—No! Go away!
(shake head no; extend arm and point out)

Turn these rocks to bread—No! Go away!
(shake head no; extend arm and point out)

Jump off of the temple—No! Go away!
(shake head no; extend arm and point out)

Bow and worship me—No! Go away!
(shake head no; extend arm and point out)

And Satan left Jesus that very day!
(shake head no; extend arm and point out)

Reader Response

Jesus Is Tempted
Matthew 4

Supplies

- "No! Go Away!" action rhyme (p. 124)

Directions

Teach the children the action rhyme "No! Go Away!" Ask the children to say the repeated phrase "No! Go away!" after you read the preceding parts. Have the children start out whispering and say the line louder each time they repeat it.

Follow Me

Two Friends Follow Jesus
John 1

Tune: "This Old Man"

Philip lived in Galilee.
Jesus said, "Come follow me."
Jesus came to Galilee
and said to him, "Come follow me."
Philip found a friend to tell.
Under a tree sat Nathaniel.
Jesus came to Galilee
and said to him, "Come follow me."
Nathaniel said, "How can it be?"
Philip answered, "Come and see!"
Jesus came to Galilee
and said to them, "Come follow me."
Soon they both followed Him.
But our story doesn't end.
Jesus wants us all to follow Him.
I will go where He will send.

Clay Name

Two Friends Follow Jesus
John 1

Children will have fun forming Jesus' name as a reminder to tell others about Him.

Supplies

- modeling clay (enough for every child to have a fist-sized ball)
- 1 cookie sheet or tray
- 1 roll of wax paper

Directions

Philip introduced Nathaniel to Jesus. We want everyone to know who Jesus is. As you sit and visit with the children, show them how to roll modeling clay into long, snake-like shapes.Form the long pieces into letters that spell Jesus' name. Lay the letters on a cookie sheet or tray for the children to see and imitate what you've done. Children can lay their letters on wax paper when they're finished.

Activity Option

Use clay that hardens as it sits out. Allow the names the children create to harden and then assist children in painting the names using various colors of tempera paint. Kids can use paintbrushes or sponges to apply the paint.

There Was a Woman

Jesus and a Woman from Samaria
John 4

There was a woman from Samaria.
(stroke hair as if it is long)

She was from a different area.
(point away from self)

Jesus asked her for a drink,
(pretend to drink from cup)

and the woman stopped to think—
(point to forehead as though thinking)

a stranger asking her for water.
(point to self)

Jesus told her about His Father.
(point up)

He talked to her about her ways.
(talking motion with hand)

She believed in Him that day.
(nod head yes)

She told her friends He knew her sins.
(point to self)

Then they believed and followed Him.
(nod head yes)

Traces of Love

Jesus and a Woman from Samaria

John 4

This tracing activity reminds children that Jesus loves all people everywhere.

Supplies

- card stock in any color (1 piece per child)
- black permanent marker
- cotton swabs
- paper cups
- water

Directions

Before class place the card stock in the horizontal position and print "Jesus Loves People Everywhere" in large letters. Repeat this on enough pieces of paper for each child in your class to have one.

During class give one sheet of card stock to each child, along with a cotton swab and a small cup of water. Do not fill the cups more than half full of water to avoid spilling. Help the children trace the preprinted words on the paper using a cotton swab dipped in water.

As the children trace the letters, tell the children that Jesus loves all people. Close with prayer thanking God for loving everyone equally.

Option for Younger Children

For younger children draw a large heart with Jesus' name written inside the outline rather than writing the words on the page.

Jesus and the Officer's Son

Jesus Heals an Official's Son

John 4

An officer of the king had a sickly son.
(rub stomach and frown)

As a worried dad he knew something must be done.
(point to temple and nod head yes)

He thought I will go to Jesus and beg Him to come with me.
(point to self and then clasp hands as though pleading)

I will go get Jesus and he went away quickly.
(point to self and then move arms up and down as though running)

Jesus did not go, but He healed the boy right then.
(shake head no; smile and nod head yes)

Jesus does great things. I'm glad He is my friend.
(smile; nod head yes; point to self)

Doctor Play Kit

Jesus Heals an Official's Son
John 4

Children will enjoy pretending to be doctors as they learn about how Jesus healed people who were sick.

Supplies

- several play doctor kits or toy medical supplies

Directions

In this activity, children can pretend to be doctors fixing imaginary injuries and helping one another.

As children play, talk with them about how wonderful it is to help someone feel better. Remind the children that Jesus didn't need medical supplies or a hospital to heal people. He healed people by the power that God gave Him.

Close with prayer, thanking God for His power to heal people.

Jesus Begins to Teach

Jesus Begins to Teach

Matthew 4

What is Jesus doing, going town to town?
(point to temple looking thoughtful)

Why does Jesus bother to travel all around?
(shrug shoulders)

Jesus is out teaching about God's wondrous love.
(cross arms over chest)

Healing all the sick with His power from above.
(point up)

People's hearts are changing, and they are saying no to sin.
(cross arms over chest; shake head no)

And they in turn tell others about Jesus their special friend.
(nod head yes; smile)

Travel and Tell

Jesus Begins to Teach
Matthew 4

This activity reminds children that all kinds of people need to know Jesus.

Supplies

- small suitcase
- images of people taken from the Internet or magazines
- red card stock (several sheets)
- scissors
- glue sticks

Directions

Before class cut out pictures from old magazines or give them pictures from the Internet of various kinds of people (i.e., elderly people, children, men, women, etc.). Cut as many hearts from the card stock as you have pictures of people. Make sure you have enough hearts and pictures so each child in your class can have at least two.

During class help children glue the people pictures onto the hearts, one picture per heart. Help the children identify what kinds of people need to know Jesus based on the pictures on the hearts (such as, men, women, children, etc.). Have children place their hearts into the suitcase as they say, "We will tell them about Jesus."

Talk with children about how Jesus traveled around to different towns, visiting with different kinds of people, to tell them about God and His love for them.

Peter, Andrew, James, and John

Fishermen Follow Jesus

Luke 5

Tune: "Deep and Wide"

Peter, Andrew, James, and John,
Peter, Andrew, James, and John,
Peter, Andrew, James, and John,
Left their nets and followed God's Son.

Peter, Andrew, James, and John,
Peter, Andrew, James, and John,
Peter, Andrew, James, and John,
Fishers of men they had become.

Jesus calls to us today.
Jesus calls to us today.
Jesus calls to us today.
He's the life, the truth, and the way.

Swish Fish

Fishermen Follow Jesus
Luke 5

These fun fish will help children remember the names of the fishermen who followed Jesus!

Supplies

- "Peter, Andrew, James, and John" Bible song (p. 134)
- copy of fish pattern (p. 212; 1 per child)
- scissors
- crayons
- washable markers

Directions

During class assist children in cutting out the fish. Using a washable marker, help the children choose and write one of the four fishermen's names on their fish: Peter, Andrew, James, or John. Allow children to color their fish as desired.

Sing the Bible song "Peter, Andrew, James, and John." During the song, have the children raise and swish their fish each time their follower's name is sung.

Here Is a Man Who Couldn't Walk

Jesus Heals a Man Who Could Not Walk

Mark 2; Luke 5

Here is a man who couldn't walk.
(hold up thumb)

Here are his friends who had a talk.
(wiggle four upright fingers)

"Carry him to Jesus!" is what they said.
(curl fingers over thumb)

So they took him on a bed.
(with fingers curled over thumb, move arm up and down in walking motion)

There was such a crowd they couldn't get through.
(shake head no)

But the four friends knew just what to do.
(point to your temple; nod head yes)

They climbed on the roof to the very top,
(put tips of fingers together to make a point)

made a hole in the roof with a chop, chop, chop.
(make an ax-chopping motion with arm and straight hand)

Down to Jesus went the man on his bed.
(thumb on palm, fingers straight out lower arm with palm facing up)

"Rise and be well" is what Jesus said.
(put thumb up)

So the man got up and went on his way.
(wave good-bye)

Jesus healed him that very day!
(smile broadly)

Rap and Roll

Jesus Heals a Man Who Could Not Walk
Mark 2; Luke 5

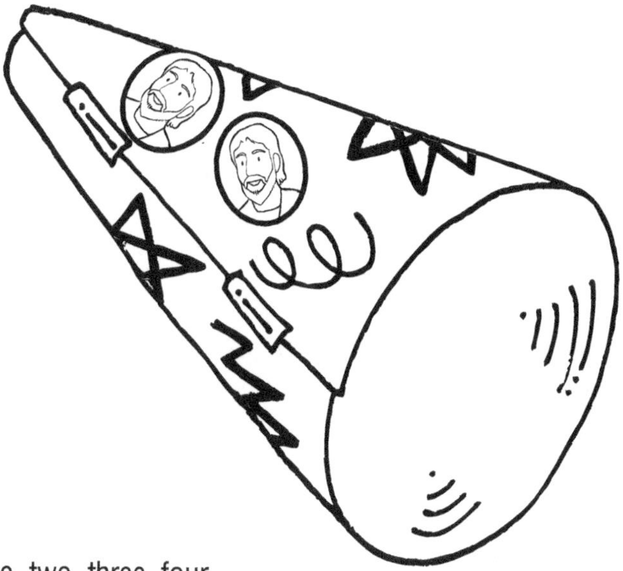

Children can use these megaphones and rap this rhyme, as they learn about Jesus healing a man who could not walk.

Supplies

- construction paper in any color (1 sheet per child)
- crayons or washable markers
- various stickers or pictures of Jesus (p. 217)
- tape
- scissors

Directions

Help children make megaphones to use as they rap the rhyme. Give each child a sheet of construction paper. Allow children to decorate their paper using crayons or washable markers and various Jesus stickers. Show children how to roll their paper into the shape of a horn or megaphone. Secure the seams with tape. Cut off any points made after rolling the paper into shape

Teach children the following rap and let them use their megaphones as they repeat the rhyme and learn about Jesus healing a man who could not walk.

One, two, three, four,

friends can't get him through the door.

Five, six, seven, eight,

go to Jesus—we can't wait!

Nine, ten, what to do?

Cut a hole and drop him through!

That's the end of this rhyme.

Jesus healed him just in time!

Matthew

Jesus and Matthew
Matthew 9

Tune: "Twinkle, Twinkle, Little Star"

Matthew, Matthew, follow me.
Leave your seat and tax money.
He went with Jesus and ate dinner.
Jesus came to save all sinners.
Matthew, Matthew, follow me.
He followed Jesus—so should we.

Follow Jesus

Jesus and Matthew
Matthew 9

Supplies

- "Matthew" Bible song (p. 138)

Directions

During class have children sit in a circle. Choose one child to play the part of Jesus.

Teach the class the Bible song "Matthew." As you sing the song, the child playing the part of Jesus should walk around the outside of the circle. When he lightly taps a seated child on the head or shoulder, that child should get up and follow "Jesus."

Continue singing and playing until all of the children are following "Jesus" as he marches around the room. Play enough times that each child has a turn playing the part of Jesus.

Praising God

Jesus Teaches about Pleasing God

Matthew 5–7

Sitting on a hillside Jesus taught a crowd one day.
(hands out as though explaining something)

He taught them how to please God—how to listen and obey.
(cup hand to ear)

Love every person, no matter what they do.
(cross arms over chest)

Love every person, the way that you love you.
(cross arms over chest; point to self)

Give to the poor, treat others kind and fair.
(arms outstretched)

He cares for everything, even birds up in the air.
(flap arms as though flying)

Do not worry, friends; please God in every way.
(shake head no; nod head yes)

Hear Jesus' words and obey them every day.
(cup hand to ear; smile; nod head yes)

Pleasing Poster

Jesus Teaches about Pleasing God
Matthew 5–7

Create this Pleasing Poster as a reminder for children that they can please God in many ways.

Supplies

- large sheet of roll paper cut your desired size
- black permanent marker
- white or light colored card stock (1 sheet per child)
- scissors or cutting board
- crayons or washable markers
- reusable adhesive or double-sided tape

Directions

Before class draw a large smile on a sheet of roll paper cut your desired size. Under the smile, write the words "We Can Please God." See the illustration. Attach the roll paper to a wall in the classroom. Cut several sheets of construction paper in half widthwise so each child has two small sheets.

During class give each child a precut sheet of card stock and crayons or washable markers. Explain to the children that they should think of a way they could please God (i.e., sharing with others, obeying their parents, helping their teacher, praying, etc.). Once each child has thought of a way to please God, he or she should write or illustrate his or her idea on the card stock. (Younger children may require additional help.)

Allow children to do this activity twice so that each child has two sheets of card stock with ways to please God either written or illustrated on them. Assist children in attaching their ideas to the large sheet of roll paper using double-sided tape or reusable adhesive.

The Widow

Jesus Teaches about Giving

Matthew 6; Mark 12

Tune: "The Farmer in the Dell"

The widow had so little,
but she gave what she had.
She gave her all and gave her best,
and that made Jesus glad.

It's not about how much
we give to God above.
He wants our hearts and gifts to be
given out of love.

Bitty Banks

Jesus Teaches about Giving
Matthew 6; Mark 12

These child-size money banks make great reminders for kids to give to God.

Supplies

- small 1¾ oz. potato chip cans with lids (1 per child)
- black permanent marker
- white paper precut into 3" x 11" strips (1 per child)
- tape
- crayons or washable markers
- utility knife

Directions

Before class cut a slit in the center of each lid large enough to drop a coin through. Using a black permanent marker, write the words "We Give" above the slit and the words "to God" below the slit.

During class pass out the precut strips of white paper to the children (1 per child) and assist them in decorating their strips using crayons or washable markers. Children can decorate these any way they like. Then help the children wrap the strips of paper around their cans and secure them using tape. Allow the children to take their Bitty Banks home as reminders to give to God.

Just Say the Word

Jesus Heals the Soldier's Servant

Matthew 8; Luke 7

Tune: "She'll Be Coming Round the Mountain"

Just say the word, my servant will be healed.
Just say the word, my servant will be healed.
Jesus, say the word, and I will leave.
He'll be healed, I do believe.
Just say the word, my servant will be healed. (Amen)

Go, for your servant has been healed today.
Go, for your servant has been healed today.
You have faith and you believe.
Now he's healed, so you may leave.
Go, for your servant has been healed today. (Amen)

Bag of Miracles

Jesus Heals the Soldier's Servant

Matthew 8; Luke 7

Children will enjoy pulling items from the Bag of Miracles as they explore the different ways Jesus healed people.

Supplies

- empty toy medical kit or first-aid kit
- pictures of eyes, ears, mouth, and legs (p. 217)
- index cards
- double-sided tape

Directions

Before class tape each picture onto an individual index card. Place all four picture cards inside a toy medical kit or first-aid kit.

During class allow one child to pull a card from the kit. Discuss the miracle that Jesus performed that the card represents: eyes represent making those who are blind to see; ears represent making those who are deaf to hear; the mouth represents making those who are mute to speak; legs represent making those who are lame to walk.

Each time select a different child to pull out a card until all four items have been selected and discussed.

Close with prayer, thanking God for having power to heal people.

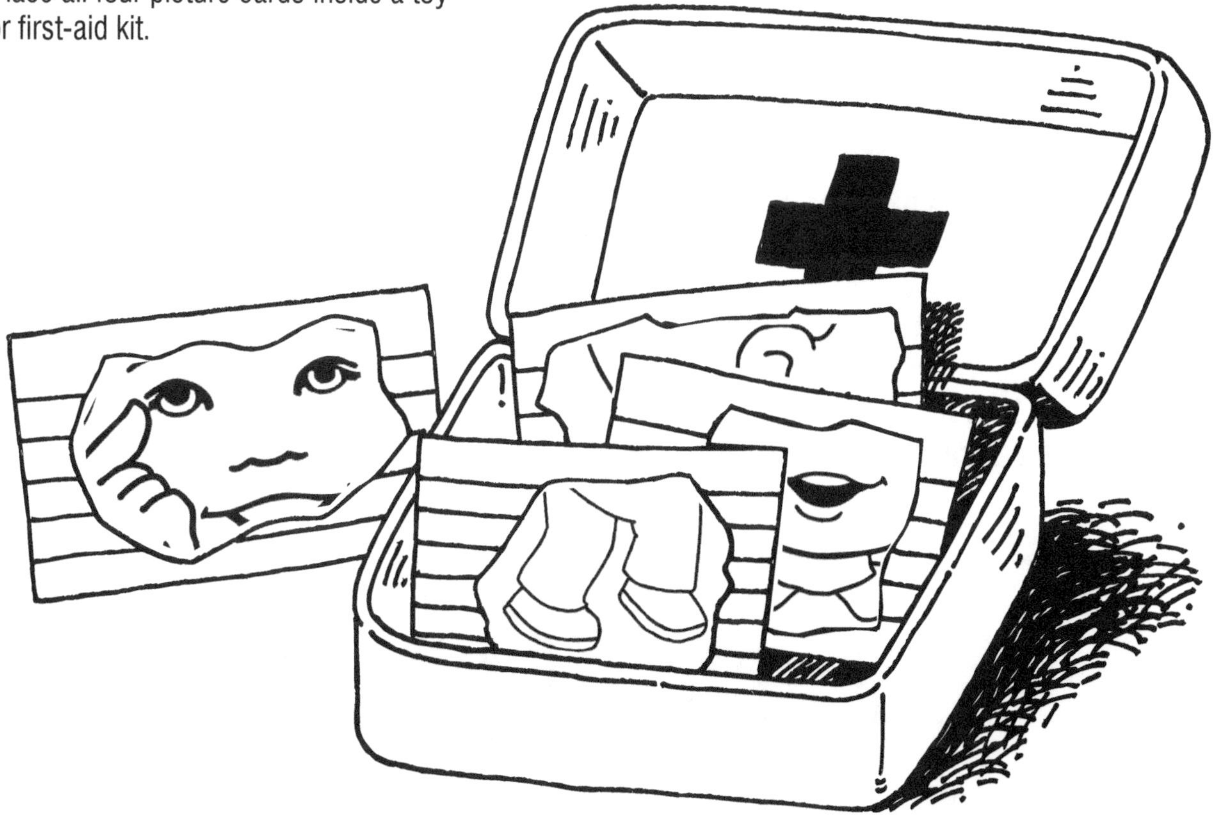

Jesus and the Widow Woman at Nain

Jesus Brings a Young Man Back to Life

Luke 7

Tune: "Reuben and Rachel"

There was once a widow woman
living in the town of Nain.
She was very sad and lonely,
and her heart was filled with pain.

Jesus saw the widow woman,
and her only son that died.
Jesus cared about that mother,
and He said to her, "Don't cry."

Jesus reached out to the young man
"Young man, get up!" Jesus said.
He sat up and spoke to Jesus,
now alive—no longer dead.

All the people crowded 'round them,
"God has come to help us out!"
Giving praise to God in heaven,
they all cheered and gave a shout.

Class Project

Jesus Brings a Young Man Back to Life

Luke 7

Supplies

- Supplies for this activity depend on the act of service you choose as a class. Read the directions below for further explanation.

Directions

Before class, select one or more widows in your congregation for whom the children in your class could do something nice as an act of service.

During class talk with the children about what a widow is and how we can serve them. Ask the children for suggestions of things they would like to do for the widows in your congregation. If children have trouble thinking of ideas, suggest some, such as making cards, visiting, or helping to clean up their yards.

Choose one act of service that you can do as a class for the widows. Remind the children that Jesus helped a widow woman by bringing her son back to life.

Close with prayer, thanking God for His power to bring people to life.

Peace, Be Still

Jesus Stops a Storm
Mark 4

Tune: "All through the Night"

Jesus in the boat is sleeping.
Peace, be still.
Though a storm winds starts a sweeping,
peace, be still.
Thunder, lightning, waves start pounding.
Disciples cry, "Jesus, we're drowning!"
Jesus wakes and calms the storm with,
"Peace, be still."

Each time you sing the phrase "Peace, be still," put your finger to your lips as though making a quiet motion.

Storm Effects

Jesus Stops a Storm
Mark 4

Supplies

- Peace, Be Still" Bible song (p. 148)
- flashlights
- aluminum pie pans

Directions

During class teach the children the Bible song "Peace, Be Still." After singing the song a few times through, pass out flashlights and aluminum pie pans to the children in your class.

Sing the song and when they come to the phrase, "Thunder, lightning, waves start pounding," allow the children to make the storm effects using their props. The pie pans can sound like thunder and the flashlights can resemble the lightning. Children without a prop can pretend to be crashing waves with their arms.

When you sing the phrase "Peace, be still," all noises should stop, just like they did when Jesus stopped the storm.

Repeat this activity several times, allowing children to trade props so that each child has a turn with each item.

Close with prayer, thanking Jesus for His power over all of creation.

Jairus's Daughter

Jesus Heals a Young Girl

Luke 8

Jairus had a daughter sick at home in bed.
(lay head on hands as though sleeping)

"I will go to Jesus" is what the ruler said.
(point to self)

"Please come and heal my daughter; please make her well today."
(clasp hands as though pleading)

The crowd along with Jesus hurried on the narrow way.
(walk fingers)

While they still were walking, someone came along and said,
(continue walking fingers)

"Don't bother Master Jesus; your daughter now is dead."
(shake head no sadly)

But Jesus told sad Jairus, "Oh, do not be afraid."
(shake head no)

They went into the bedroom where the sickly young girl laid.
(lay head on hands as though sleeping)

"Stand up, my child," said Jesus as He took her by the hand.
(extend hand)

Then opening her eyes, she quickly took a stand.
(two fingers down on palm as though standing)

Her parents were amazed and the word spread in an hour.
(smile)

Jesus is God's Son, and He has a mighty power!
(flex muscles like a strong man)

Helping Center

Jesus Heals a Young Girl
Luke 8

Create this interactive learning center to help children remember that Jesus was able to help people with God's help.

Supplies

- doll beds
- blankets
- dolls
- toy medical kits
- toy rescue vehicles
- firefighter hats
- various items or apparel that represent medical and emergency personnel

Directions

Before class create a helping center where kids can play. Place items in the learning center for kids to use as they pretend to help people in need.

During class allow the children to play in the helping center and pretend to help each other.

Discuss how medical and emergency personnel use equipment to help people. But Jesus has the power to heal people right away without the use of tools or equipment. Jesus heals people by God's power.

Close with prayer, thanking God for helping us and praise Him for His power to heal people.

Five Little Loaves

Jesus Feeds a Crowd
John 6

Tune: "Hush, Little Baby"

Five little loaves and two little fish,
one small boy and a great big wish
to hear Jesus from a hillside rock.
He followed Jesus with his lunch box.

A large crowd of people came that day
to hear Jesus and learn His ways.
The crowd grew hungry and needed fed.
The only food was fish and bread.

To Jesus this boy gave his lunch.
Just a little, but soon was much.
Jesus prayed and blessed the bread;
then 5,000 folks were fed.

Jesus is God's special one.
He's God's one and only Son.
He can do many wonderful things!
He's the reason that we sing!

Let's Do Lunch

Jesus Feeds a Crowd
John 6

Supplies

- "Five Little Loaves" Bible song (p. 152)
- lunch box
- 5 pieces of bread or crackers
- 2 toy fish

Directions

Teach the children the Bible song "Five Little Loaves." As you sing the first verse, place the bread or crackers and the two toy fish into the lunch box and close the lid. At the end of the second verse, open the lunch box and show the fish and bread. On the third verse, act as though you're passing out the lunch to each child.

Repeat the song, allowing the children to take turns acting out the song with the lunch box.

Talk with the children about how we can share what we have with God and with others.

Row, Row, Row the Boat

Jesus Walks on Water
Mark 6; John 6

Tune: "Row, Row, Row Your Boat"

Row, row, row the boat; it is getting late.
Now the wind is blowing hard; oh, the waves are great!

Jesus sees His friends struggle with the boat.
They are rowing very hard, trying to stay afloat.

Who's that walking there on Lake Galilee?
Walking on the water—It is Jesus! Can it be?

Jesus walks to them right across the sea.
Jesus is all-powerful—the Son of God is He!

Rowing Role Play

Jesus Walks on Water
Mark 6; John 6

Supplies

- "Row, Row, Row the Boat" Bible song (p. 154)
- large, long, open cardboard box
- roll of blue crepe paper
- scissors

Directions

Before class cut the blue crepe paper into sections that are each two feet long. Cut enough sections so that each child can have one.

During class choose children to play Jesus, the disciples in the boat, and the waves in the water. Choose several children to play the waves. Give them streamers made from blue crepe paper.

Begin the role play by asking "disciples" to sit in a box, which represents a boat. They should pretend to row the boat. The children playing the part of the waves should wave their crepe paper streamers and make sound effects of howling, blowing wind.

The child playing the part of Jesus should walk through the "waves" toward the "boat." He or she should tell "the disciples" not to be afraid. As "Jesus" steps into the boat, the "waves" should stop all sound and movement.

Once the children are comfortable with the role play, teach them the Bible song "Row, Row, Row the Boat." Allow the children to act out the song as they have practiced.

Once There Was a Man

Jesus Heals a Man Who Could Not Hear or Speak
Mark 7

Once there was a man who could not hear or talk.
(point to ear; point to mouth)

His friends brought him to Jesus. Walk, walk, walk, walk, walk.
(march in place)

Jesus took the man out from the busy crowd.
(reach out; grab with hand; pull back)

He touched his ears and mouth and said these words aloud,
(point to ears; point to mouth)

"Be opened!" and the man was healed. But Jesus said, "Don't tell."
(shake finger as though telling someone not to do something)

But the people could not help it and said, "He does all things well!"
(shake head no; arms out as though explaining something)

Charades

Jesus Heals a Man Who Could Not Hear or Speak
Mark 7

Directions
During class ask children to list simple tasks they do throughout the day (talking on the phone, brushing teeth, watching TV, eating meals, etc.).

Talk with children about what it would be like to not be able to hear or speak. As a class, silently act out the simple tasks they listed. Remind them that they should act them out as though they cannot hear or speak.

When you're finished ask children to tell which activities were difficult, which were not difficult, and which were impossible (talking on the phone, etc.).

Remind the children that Jesus helped a man who could not hear or speak by healing him.

Close with prayer thanking God for caring about everyone and praising Him for His power to heal people.

Jesus Is All-Powerful

Jesus Heals a Man Born Blind
John 9

Tune: "London Bridge"

Jesus is all-powerful, powerful, powerful.
Jesus is all-powerful. He made a blind man see.
Jesus is all-powerful, powerful, powerful.
Jesus is all-powerful. He can sure help me.

Eye Prints

Jesus Heals a Man Born Blind
John 9

These colorful Eye Prints remind kids that Jesus has teh power to make those who are blind see!

Supplies

- package of 6" coated paper plates
- washable markers
- Silly Putty modeling clay (preferably coral colored)

Directions

Before class draw pairs of eyes in the center of several paper plates using washable markers. Draw one pair per plate. Be sure to alternate through eye colors on the plates by using brown, blue, and green markers. Make enough plates for each child in the class to have one.

During class show the children how to work with modeling clay until it is flexible. Help the children flatten the clay to make a thin, pancake like oval. Assist children in placing their putty on top of the eyes on the plates and help them press down. Help children carefully remove the clay. Colorful eye prints should show on the underneath side of the putty.

Talk with children about how Jesus put mud on the eyes of a man born blind and about how Jesus had the power to make him see.

I'll Help and Do My Part

Jesus Teaches about Helping

Matthew 7; Luke 10

Tune: "This Old Man"

I will help and do my part,
have a kind and willing heart.
I'll show God's love with my helping hands;
be a good Samaritan.

I will help and do my part,
have a kind and willing heart.
I'll show God's love and do what I can do;
be a helping friend to you.

I will help and do my part,
have a kind and willing heart.
I will be a friend to everyone;
I want to be like God's Son.

I will help and do my part,
have a kind and willing heart.
I'll show God's love with my helping hands;
be a good Samaritan.

Helping Heart

Jesus Teaches about Helping
Matthew 7; Luke 10

Children learn about helping others as they take turns looking inside the Helping Heart while singing the Bible song "I'll Help and Do My Part."

Supplies

- "I'll Help and Do My Part" Bible song (p. 160)
- empty heart-shaped box
- 2 pictures showing children helping someone (cut from a magazine or taken from the Internet)
- double-sided tape

Directions

Before class cut two pictures from a newspaper or magazine showing children helping someone. Cut the pictures to fit inside the heart-shaped box and tape them in place, one on each side inside the box.

During class sing the Bible song "I'll Help and Do My Part." During the song show the heart closed and then open the heart to show the pictures inside.

After the song, talk with the children about helping others. Ask children to name ways they can be helpers.

Activity Option

After this activity continue the lesson on helping by creating a classroom helper chart. Assign a different task to each child (pushing in chairs, picking up extra paper, putting away extra toys, etc.) and list children's names and their specific tasks on the chart. Hang the chart in the classroom. For variety, change the tasks around each time your class meets so that each child has an opportunity to help in every way.

This Is Mary; This Is Martha

Mary and Martha Follow Jesus
Luke 10

Tune: "Frere Jacques"

This is Mary; this is Martha,
Jesus' friends, Jesus' friends.
Mary hears Jesus; Martha serves Jesus.
They love Him. They love Him.

Mary listens; Martha serves
friend Jesus, friend Jesus.
Martha makes a good choice; Mary makes the best choice.
Listen to Him. Listen to Him.

Helping Hands

Mary and Martha Follow Jesus
Luke 10

Supplies

- "This Is Mary, This Is Martha" Bible song (p. 162)

Directions

During class teach the children the Bible song "This Is Mary, This Is Martha." Repeat the song several times until children are comfortable with the words.

Teach children the following motions to the song: hold up one index finger for Mary and one for Martha. Place the Mary finger next to your ear when you sing the phrase about Mary hearing Jesus. Use the Martha finger to point at your other hand when you sing the phrase about Martha serving Jesus.

When you sing *love*, cross both arms over your chest. Smile when you sing *good choice* and nod your head when you sing *best choice*.

Allow children to take turns leading the motions for the rest of the class.

Talk to God

Jesus Teaches about Praying

Matthew 6; Luke 11

Tune: "Row, Row, Row Your Boat"

Talk, talk, talk to God.
Talk to God today.
Bow your head and close your eyes
and talk to God today.

Listen to His words.
Listen to His words.
Hear His words and then obey.
Listen to His words.

Table Talk Prayers

Jesus Teaches about Praying
Matthew 6; Luke 11

Supplies

- white roll paper
- masking tape
- crayons or washable markers

Directions

Before class cover the table surface with white roll paper. Secure it under the edges of the table using masking tape.

During class talk with the children about how Jesus prayed. Ask the children if they have someone or something they would like to pray for or about. Allow children to think for a few moments.

Pass out crayons or washable markers. Allow children to draw their prayer concerns on the table paper. Younger children may need help with this activity. You may also encourage them to draw what we can thank God for.

Talk with the children about how we can pray to God and remind them that God always hears our prayers. Show children how to bow their heads and fold their hands to prepare for prayer time. Tell children that we do this to show respect for God and to help us to not be distracted by other things when we pray.

Close with prayer, mentioning each of the requests that the children have illustrated on the table paper. Invite other children to pray as well. If children want to pray but cannot think of what to say, offer to pray and allow them to repeat your words.

Greedy Farmer

Jesus Teaches about Sharing
Luke 12

I grow much food here on my farm.
(pretend to rake)

There's too much food for my small barns.
(open arms wide; hands close together as though showing a small space)

Build bigger barns—for me I care.
(point to self)

But God's not pleased when we don't share.
(shake head no)

I'll share and care as Jesus would.
(nod head yes)

I'll do the things I know I should.
(point to side of head)

I'll share my toys and take my turn.
(extend arm and hand)

I'll read God's Word and pray and learn.
(open hands like a book; fold hands as though praying)

Sharing Shakers

Jesus Teaches about Sharing
Luke 12

These fun shakers help kids learn about sharing as they shake to the rhythm of the action rhyme about the greedy farmer.

Supplies

- "Greedy Farmer" action rhyme (p. 166)
- inexpensive plastic fruit or vegetables (1 per child)
- scissors or a sharp knife
- popcorn kernels or dry rice
- colored duct tape

Directions

Before class carefully poke a small hole in the end of each piece of fruit or each vegetable using scissors or a sharp knife. Place a small handful of popcorn kernels or dry rice inside each piece of fruit or vegetable and seal the hole using duct tape.

During class teach children the action rhyme about the greedy farmer. As children learn the rhyme, show them how to keep a beat using the sharing shakers.

Close with prayer, asking God to help you learn to share with others.

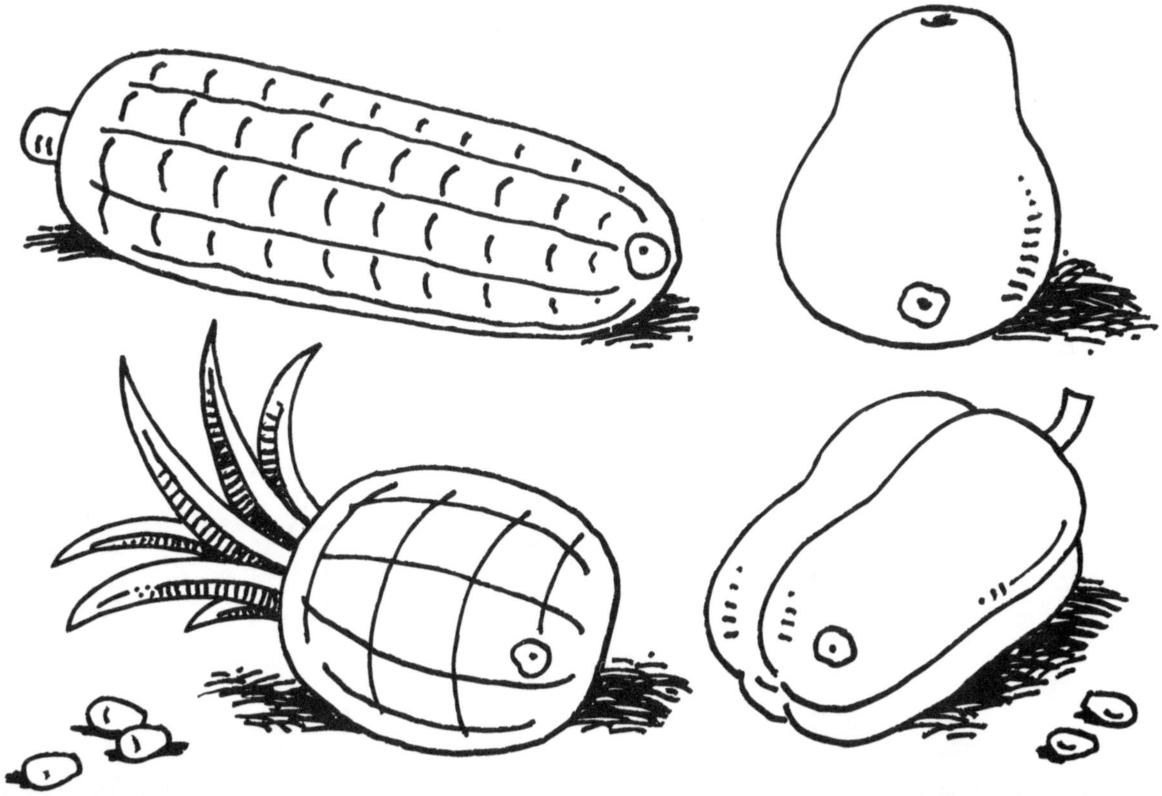

Lazarus Is Alive

Jesus Brings Lazarus Back to Life
John 11

Tune: "Bingo"

He was dead but now he's not.
Oh, Lazarus is alive-o!

Chorus
A-L-I-V-E, A-L-I-V-E, A-L-I-V-E,
Oh, Lazarus is alive-o!

In the tomb for four long days
but now he is alive-o!

Repeat chorus

God has power over death.
Oh, Lazarus is alive-o!

Repeat chorus

Jesus is God's mighty Son.
Oh, Lazarus is alive-o!

Repeat chorus

Letter Cards

Jesus Brings Lazarus Back to Life
John 11:

Supplies

- "Lazarus Is Alive" Bible song (p. 168)
- 3 manila folders
- scissors
- black permanent marker

Directions

Before class cut three manila folders in half along the fold line. Write on each card one letter of the word *alive*. On the last card, write an exclamation point.

During class teach the children the Bible song "Lazarus Is Alive." Choose six children to help you. Give each child one of the cards. Line the children up in front of the class so that their cards spell out the word *alive* with the exclamation point card at the end of the word.

As you sing the song, point to each child when his letter is sung to signal when he is to raise his card. The child holding the exclamation point should raise his card on the phrase "Oh, Lazarus is alive-o!"

Repeat the song, allowing all of the children to have a turn holding a card.

One Healed Leper

Jesus Heals Ten Men
Luke 17

Tune: "Praise Him, Praise Him, All Ye Little Children"

Thank Him, thank Him, one healed leper.
He said thanks. He said thanks.
Thank Him, thank Him, one healed leper.
He said thanks. He said thanks.

Thank-You Cards

Jesus Heals Ten Men
Luke 17

Supplies

- card stock in various colors (1 sheet per child)
- wallpaper sample book
- double-sided tape
- black permanent marker
- decorative embellishments: dollies, ribbon, trim, buttons, feathers, etc. *(optional)*

Directions

Before class cut several pieces of wallpaper from a wallpaper sample book. Fold the wallpaper to form the outside of a card. Fold the card stock in half and place it inside the wallpaper cover. You may want to trim the cover to be slightly larger than the card stock inside. Staple the two pieces together along the top and bottom of the fold line. Write "Thank You" on the inside of each card.

During class help the children decide who they would like to send thank-you cards to and then allow them to decorate their cards. Make sure that the class considers people who may not get thanked often for what they do, like janitors and nursery workers.

Talk with children about how the people whom Jesus helped were most likely very thankful for what He did for them. Remind the children that we need to remember as well to be thankful for everything God does for us. And we need to say thank you to others when they help us too.

If it is possible, go as a class to deliver your thank-you cards.

Close with prayer, thanking God for helping people and praising Him for His power to not only heal people but also to bring people back to life!

Jesus, Friend of Little Children

Jesus and the Children
Mark 10

Tune: "Jesus Loves the Little Children"

Jesus, friend of little children—
every child, everywhere.
He loves us each and everyone.
Jesus is God's only Son.
Jesus is a friend to children everywhere.

God Loves the World

Jesus and the Children
Mark 10

Supplies

- "Jesus, Friend of Little Children" Bible song (p. 172)
- small spinning globe or large map

Directions

During class sing the Bible song "Jesus, Friend of Little Children." Pass the globe around among the children as you sing. Allow each child to take a turn spinning the globe and looking at all of the different places shown or point to places on the map.

Talk with the children about how Jesus loves all children—boys and girls from everywhere in the world and with every color of skin, hair, and eyes.

Close with prayer, thanking God for making each person so unique and special and for loving everyone equally.

Bartimaeus

Bartimaeus Follows Jesus

Mark 10; Luke 18

Sitting in Jericho with no place to go,
(shake head no)

Bartimaeus was begging on the side of the road.
(place hand out)

People were talking and word got around,
(pretend to whisper)

the man they call Jesus was coming to town!
(point into the distance)

Everyone gathered to hear what He'd say.
(cup hand at ear)

Bartimaeus cried out as Jesus passed his way.
(cup hands at mouth as though shouting)

The people with Jesus shushed the man, blind and poor.
(place finger at mouth)

But he would not listen and cried out even more.
(shake head no; cup hands at mouth)

He cried out real loud, "Jesus, please help me!"
(point out; point at self)

"I want more than anything to be able to see!"
(point to eyes)

Jesus replied, "Because you believe,"
(nod head yes)

"Your faith has healed you" and the man started to see!
(point to eyes)

The whole crowd was happy Bartimaeus was well.
(smile and nod head yes)

Bartimaeus followed Jesus with a story to tell!
(walk fingers on palm)

Footprint Follow

Bartimaeus Follows Jesus
Mark 10; Luke 18

Supplies

- card stock (1 sheet per child)
- washable markers
- scissors
- masking tape or reusable adhesive
- picture of Jesus
- scarf or blindfold
- copy of Footprint Follow art of Jesus (p. 216)

Directions

This is a spin on the traditional game of Pin the Tail on the Donkey. Before you play, have each child trace and cut out one footprint. Encourage the children to help each other trace one another's feet. For younger children you may want to prepare these footprints before class.

Write each child's name on one side of his footprint and place a loop of masking tape or reusable adhesive on the other side. Place a picture of Jesus on the wall at the eye level of the children.

Take turns blindfolding each child. Spin the blindfolded child around a few times and point him in the direction of the picture of Jesus. The object of the game is to get the footprints as close to the picture of Jesus as possible.

Make sure you remove the surrounding area any objects that have sharp edges where children could get hurt if they were to bump into them.

Play the game long enough for each child to have a turn being blindfolded.

Zacchaeus

Jesus and Zacchaeus
Luke 19

Here is a tree growing so tall;
(bend right arm at elbow; spread fingers)

Here is a man so short and so small.
(raise left index finger)

Look! It's Zacchaeus and he's up in the tree!
(move index finger up arm to fingers/branches)

Jesus is coming, and Zacchaeus wants to see!
(nod head yes; point to eyes)

Then Jesus looked up in that sycamore tree,
(place hand over eyes as though searching)

And said to Zacchaeus, "Come down here to me."
(cup hands at mouth)

I'm going to your house. Yes, this very day,
(put fingertips together to make roof)

I'm going to your house, and that's where I'll stay!"
(point out; nod head yes and smile)

Time with Jesus

Jesus and Zacchaeus
Luke 19

Directions
In the Bible story, Jesus went to stay at the home of Zacchaeus. Talk with the children about what it's like when guests come to visit. Ask the children to think of some things they would make to eat if they knew Jesus was coming to their homes. Ask them to explore what they might talk about with Jesus. How might they behave?

While Jesus stayed with Zacchaeus, they probably talked to one another. Ask the children to now consider what Jesus might say to them if He were to come to stay at their homes.

Allow the children to share their responses to these questions with the class.

Close with prayer, thanking God for being so loving and for wanting to spend time with the people He made.

Jesus Enters Jerusalem

A Crowd Welcomes Jesus
Matthew 21

Tune: "When the Saints Go Marching In"

Jesus enters Jer-u-sa-lem.
Jesus enters Jer-u-sa-lem.
Oh, Jesus rides a little donkey
entering Jer-u-sa-lem.

Oh, spread your coats and wave your palms.
Spread your coats and wave your palms.
Shout "Praise to God in heaven!"
Spread your coats and wave your palms.

Donkey Clop

A Crowd Welcomes Jesus
Matthew 21

Supplies

- "Jesus Enters Jerusalem" Bible song (p. 178)
- rhythm sticks or wood blocks

Directions

During class teach the children the Bible song "Jesus Enters Jerusalem." Once the children are comfortable with the words and the tune, pass out rhythm sticks or wood blocks.

Sing the Bible song again, this time allowing the children to use their rhythm instruments to make the sounds of a donkey's feet on a road like the sound Jesus might have heard as He rode into Jerusalem. Show the children how to tap the sticks or blocks together to make the noise and how to keep a steady beat.

Oh, Come and Sing

People Praise Jesus
Mark 11

Tune: "The Farmer in the Dell"

Oh, come and sing along.
Oh, come and sing along.
We'll wave some palms and sing some songs.
Oh, come and sing along.

The girls will sing along.
The girls will sing along.
They'll wave their palms and sing some songs.
The girls will sing along.

The boys will sing along.
The boys will sing along.
They'll wave their palms and sing some songs.
The boys will sing along.

We'll lay our branches down.
We'll lay our branches down.
We'll lay our coats and branches down
as Jesus rides to town.

Divide the children into two groups (one girls' group and one boys' group). The teacher should sing the first verse of the song. The girls should sing the second verse, and the boys should sing the third verse. Everyone should join together to sing the final verse.

Do the Wave

People Praise Jesus
Mark 11

Supplies

- palm branches
- various garments (bathrobes, oversize shirts, miscellaneous pieces of fabric, etc.)
- toy horse or broom

Directions

Using the supplies listed above, reenact the triumphal entry. Select some children to lay down various garments on a path that you've created in your classroom. Select other children to wave palm branches and cheer. Select one child to pretend to ride a colt along the path as Jesus did.

Reenact the story several times, each time allowing children to change roles. Make sure each child has an opportunity to play the part of Jesus at least once.

Early Sunday Morning

Jesus Is Alive!
Matthew 28

Early Sunday morning while most were sound asleep,
(yawn)

Mary and Mary softly to the tomb did creep.
(finger to lips)

Sitting on the stone that had been rolled away,
(rolling motion with hands)

an angel flashed like lightning, shining bright as day.
(place back of hand over eyes)

"Do not be afraid, now put away your fear."
(shake head no)

"Jesus rose up from the dead and now He is not here."
(raise hands from low to high; shake head no)

"Go quickly and tell His followers,"
(point into distance)

"'Go into Galilee.'
(cup hands at mouth)

"'He has risen from the dead, so hurry come and see.'"
(motion to come with hand)

Son Flowers

Jesus Is Alive!
Matthew 28

In this activity, every flower becomes a Son Flower as it helps kids tell others that Jesus is alive!

Supplies

- white foam cups (1 per child)
- permanent markers in any color
- darning needle
- washable markers
- Easter or spring stickers
- small plants (petunias or marigolds work well; 1 per child)
- bag of potting soil
- water
- small plastic lids

Directions

Before class use permanent markers to write the words, "Jesus Is Alive!" on each foam cup. Using a darning needle, put holes in the bottom of the cup for drainage.

During class give each child a foam cup and allow them to decorate the cups using washable markers and various resurrection Sunday or spring stickers. Once the cups are decorated, add potting soil to each child's cup. Help each child place a small plant into his cup and add a small amount of water. Set the cups on small plastic lids to catch water that leaks from the cups.

Children can use their flowers as reminders to tell others that new life comes in the springtime and Jesus is alive too!

Jesus Lives Again

Jesus Lives!
John 21

Tune: "The Farmer in the Dell"

Jesus lives again.
Jesus lives again.
Alive and well,
oh, go and tell,
Jesus lives again!

Jesus helps His friends.
Jesus helps His friends.
Toss your net
and fish you'll get.
Jesus helps His friends.

Jesus cares for friends.
Jesus cares for friends.
He cooked some fish
oh, tasty dish.
Jesus cares for friends.

Fish Fry Game

Jesus Lives!
John 21

Play this fun game with children as a reminder that Jesus cooked fish for His followers after He rose from the dead.

Supplies

- "Jesus Lives Again" Bible song (p. 184)
- toy fish, beanbag, or Swish Fish (p. 212) printed on card stock

Directions

During class teach the children the Bible song "Jesus Lives Again." Have the children sit in a circle. As you sing the song, pass the fish around the circle. When the song is finished, the person left holding the fish should move to the center of the circle, or, the "frying pan". Continue the game until all of the children are in the "frying pan." The last child left is named the fish fryer.

What Shall We Do?

Peter Preaches about Jesus

Acts 2

Tune: "Happy Birthday"

How did the church start?
How did the church start?
With wind, fire, and preaching,
that's how it did start.

Peter, what shall we do?
Peter, what shall we do?
Change your ways and be baptized;
that's what you must do!

So that's what they did.
So that's what they did.
Three thousand were saved;
that's what the church did.

Celebrate the Church

Peter Preaches about Jesus
Acts 2

Supplies

- cake
- paper plates
- plastic forks
- napkins
- decorations

Directions

As a class, throw a celebration party for the church! Make the party as elaborate as you like. Feel free to send invitations—children can even help make these prior to the party! Decorate the classroom, play games, and, of course, enjoy some cake! Don't forget to have everyone wash their hands.

Talk with children about what happened on the day Peter addressed a crowd and 3,000 people chose to follow Jesus.

Close with prayer, thanking God for sending His Son to earth.

Care and Share

The Church Follows Jesus

Acts 2, 4

Tune: "Frere Jacques"

Care and share.
Care and share.
The church cared.
The church shared.
They shared their homes and family.
They shared their food and money.
They loved God.
They loved God.

Care and share.
Care and share.
I can care.
I can share.
I can share with friends at church.
I can share with family.
I love God.
I love God.

Share a Snack

The Church Follows Jesus
Acts 2, 4

Supplies

- "Care and Share" Bible song (p. 188)
- ingredients to make a snack mix (cereal squares, pretzels, chocolate pieces, raisins, etc.)
- resealable bags
- bowl
- spoon
- plastic scoop

Directions

During class talk with children about how the early Christians shared their possessions with one another. Help the children share with others by making a special snack for a group in your congregation.

After the children wash their hands, allow them to take turns adding the ingredients in the supplies list to the bowl and stirring them together. Children can then use a plastic scoop to place the mixture in resealable bags. Deliver the snacks as a class if possible. During the delivery, sing the Bible song "Care and Share."

Remember to check with parents about food allergies.

In the Name

Peter and John at the Temple
Acts 3

Tune: "She'll Be Coming Round the Mountain"

In the name of Jesus Christ, go walk about.
In the name of Jesus Christ, go walk about.
In Jesus' name, go walk about.
Jump for joy and give a shout.
In the name of Jesus Christ, go walk about.

In the name of Jesus Christ, go jump for joy.
In the name of Jesus Christ, go jump for joy.
In Jesus' name, go jump for joy.
Then tell every girl and boy,
in the name of Jesus Christ, go jump for joy.

In the name of Jesus Christ, oh praise the Lord.
In the name of Jesus Christ, oh praise the Lord.
We will sing and pray to Him.
Jesus is our special friend.
In the name of Jesus Christ, oh praise the Lord!

Peter Says

Peter and John at the Temple
Acts 3

Directions

Play a variation of the game Simon Says. This game is Peter Says! Choose one child to play the part of Peter. This child should lead the class in motions that they must imitate if he uses the words "Peter says" before saying the action. If the child leading the game has trouble thinking of actions to call out, offer some simple ideas such as asking the class to place their hands on their feet, ankles, knees, legs, heads, etc. Remind the children that if the leader does not say "Peter says" before an action, they should not imitate the action. If they do, they must sit down.

Play the game several times, allowing each child to have a turn being the leader.

Reading While Riding

Philip Tells about Jesus
Acts 8

Tune: "Go Tell Aunt Rhody"

He's reading to himself.
He's reading to himself.
He's reading to himself—
not sure about the scroll.

Philip ran to catch him.
Philip ran to catch him.
Philip ran to catch him
and teach him from the scroll.

Philip taught that man.
Philip taught that man.
Philip taught that man,
starting with the scroll.

Tell about Jesus.
Tell about Jesus.
Tell about Jesus,
the Bible is our scroll.

Story Scrolls

Philip Tells about Jesus
Acts 8

These scrolls remind children that Philip told others about Jesus and are helpful tools kids can use to tell others too!

Supplies

- white paper (1 piece per child)
- crayons or washable markers
- plastic straws (2 per child)
- tape
- rubber bands (1 per child)

Directions

Lay a piece of paper in the horizontal position on a table in front of each child. Help the children draw a scene from the story found in Acts 8:26–40 of Philip telling about Jesus. When the drawings are complete, tape a straw to each end of the papers and show the children how to roll each end toward the center to make a scroll. Secure the scroll using a rubber band.

Children can take their Story Scrolls home and use them as they share with their families and friends the story of Philip telling about Jesus.

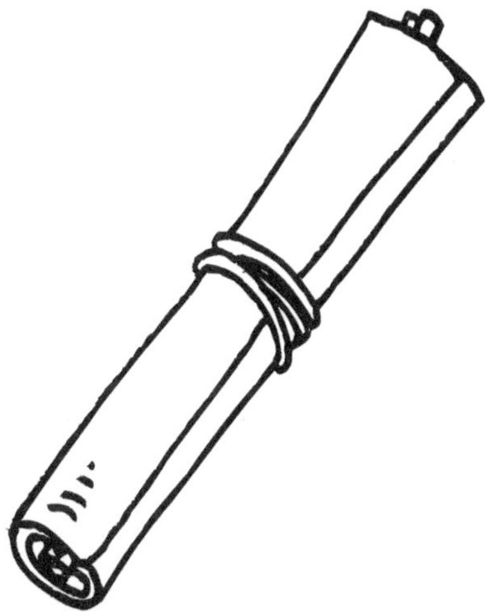

A Shiny Light Flashed 'Round

Saul Begins to Follow Jesus
Acts 9

Tune: "This Little Light of Mine"

A shiny light flashed 'round; Saul fell to the ground.
A shiny light flashed 'round; Saul fell to the ground.
A shiny light flashed 'round; Saul fell to the ground,
to the ground, to the ground, to the ground.

Then a voice rang out, "Saul! Saul" it shouts.
Then a voice rang out, "Saul! Saul" it shouts.
Then a voice rang out, "Saul! Saul" it shouts,
it shouts, it shouts, it shouts.

"Oh, who are You, Lord?" "I am Jesus Christ."
"Oh, who are You, Lord?" "I am Jesus Christ."
"Oh, who are You, Lord?" "I am Jesus Christ."
Jesus Christ, Jesus Christ, Jesus Christ.

Now blinded by the light, Saul did not have sight.
Now blinded by the light, Saul did not have sight.
Now blinded by the light, Saul did not have sight,
no sight, no sight, no sight.

Saul prayed and did not eat. Ananias he did meet.
Saul prayed and did not eat. Ananias he did meet.
Saul prayed and did not eat. Ananias he did meet,
did meet, did meet, did meet.

Now healed he saw again, took Jesus as his friend.
Now healed he saw again, took Jesus as his friend.
Now healed he saw again, took Jesus as his friend,
as his friend, as his friend, as his friend.

Sing and Shine

Saul Begins to Follow Jesus
Acts 9

Supplies

- "A Shiny Light Flashed 'Round" Bible song (p. 194)
- working flashlights (1 per child)

Directions

During class teach children the Bible song "A Shiny Light Flashed 'Round." Once children have practiced the song a few times, give each child a flashlight. Turn down the lights in the classroom and sing the Bible song.

Talk with children about the light that blinded Saul on his way to Damascus.

Tabitha

Peter and Tabitha
Acts 9

Tune: "Kum-Bah-Yah"

Oh, Ta-bi-tha loved the Lord.
Oh, Ta-bi-tha loved the Lord.
She helped the poor with clothes and more.
Ta-bi-tha loved the Lord.

Oh, Ta-bi-tha became sick.
Oh, Ta-bi-tha became sick.
And when she died, the people cried.
Ta-bi-tha became sick.

Oh, Ta-bi-tha was loved by friends.
Oh, Ta-bi-tha was loved by friends.
Have Peter come, oh quickly run.
Ta-bi-tha was loved by friends.

Oh, Ta-bi-tha, get up, get up!
Oh, Ta-bi-tha, get up, get up!
When Peter spoke, she awoke.
Ta-bi-tha, get up, get up!

Oh, Ta-bi-tha is alive.
Oh, Ta-bi-tha is alive.
She was raised, so shout your praise.
Ta-bi-tha is alive.

Stage a Stanza

Peter and Tabitha
Acts 9

Supplies

- "Tabitha" Bible song (p. 196)
- heart shape cut from red card stock
- shirt or robe
- tissues
- copy of artwork of Jesus (p. 216)

Directions

During class teach children the Bible song "Tabitha." Once children are familiar with the song, act out each of the five verses as a class.

For the first verse, choose one child to hold the red heart and another child to show the shirt or robe to the rest of the class. In the second verse, several children should dab their eyes with the tissues as they pretend to cry. In the third verse, one child should act as Peter and should run in place. In the fourth verse, one child should stretch and yawn. In the last verse, one child should hold a picture of Jesus.

Split up the parts so that each child in the class has something to do during the song.

Who's That Knocking?

The Church Prays for Peter in Prison
Acts 12

Tune: "Little Liza Jane"

Who's that knocking at the door?
Peter's out there.

Who's that knocking at the door?
Peter's out there.

Oh, dear Rhoda,
Peter's out there.

Oh, dear Rhoda,
open the door.

Who is praying for Peter?
Church friends pray there.

Who is praying for Peter?
Church friends pray there.

Oh, dear church friends,
Peter's out there.

Oh, dear church friends,
God answers prayer.

Knocking Blocks

The Church Prays for Peter in Prison
Acts 12

Supplies

- wood blocks or rhythm sticks (2 sets)

Directions

Talk with children about what happened when the church prayed for Peter while he was in prison and how an angel led him out of the cell in the middle of the night. As a class, act out what happened next when Peter showed up at Rhoda's house.

Choose one child to be Peter. This child will pretend to knock on a door using the wood blocks or rhythm sticks to make the knocking sound. Choose another child to be Rhoda. She should pretend to run to the door. She can use wood blocks or rhythm sticks to make the sound of running feet. The other children can pretend to be the church members inside the house praying for Peter.

Remind the child playing Rhoda that after she goes to the door and hears Peter's voice outside, she should run back to the other church members and tell them the news without opening the door first because she's so surprised. The other children should pretend not to believer her that Peter is outside.

Repeat this activity several times, each time choosing two new children to play the parts of Peter and Rhoda.

Lydia

Lydia Follows Jesus

Acts 16

Tune: "Looby Lou"

Chorus
Lydia sold fine cloth
made with a purple dye.
Lydia heard Paul teach
down by the riverside.

Down by the riverside
women gathered there.
Lydia came to worship
and talk to God in prayer.

Repeat chorus

Jesus is God's Son,
was taught by Paul that day.
Oh, Lydia believed in Him,
the truth, the life, the way.

Repeat chorus

Lydia had great joy.
God's love she had to share.
Invited Paul to use her home
'till he was finished there.

Repeat chorus

Lydia Loopers

Lydia Follows Jesus
Acts 16

Children will enjoy making and waving these loopers as they sing songs about Lydia.

Supplies

- "Lydia" Bible song (p. 200)
- 18" strips of purple crepe paper (2 or 3 per child)
- packing tape
- large craft sticks or (1 per child)

Directions

Before class cut purple crepe paper into strips that are each 18" long.

During class give each child a craft stick or ruler and two or three precut strips of crepe paper. Assist children in taping one end of the crepe paper strips to the end of the craft sticks. Each child can wave his or her Lydia looper through the air as you sing the Bible song "Lydia."

Tell the children that the Bible says Lydia sold purple cloth. The loopers can serve as a reminder for children that Lydia followed God and we can too.

We're Here!

The Jailer Follows Jesus
Acts 16

Tune: "My Bonnie Lies over the Ocean"

In prison sat Paul and Silas;
though beaten they sang and they prayed.
God heard them and sent a great earthquake—
Doors opened and chains fell away.

Chorus
We're here! We're here!
Oh, jailer, do yourself no harm, no harm.
We're here! We're here!
Oh, jailer, do yourself no harm!

The jailer rushed into the prison,
And shouted for torches, "Come fast!"
He saw all the prisoners were still there,
each one from the first to the last.

Repeat chorus

The jailer was shaking and frightened.
So he asked Paul, "What must I do?"
"Believe in God's Son, the Lord Jesus."
He did and his family did too!

Repeat chorus

The jailer and family were baptized,
right then, though the hour was late.
So joy-filled they helped Paul and Silas.
Isn't our God really great?

Repeat chorus

In Chains

The Jailer Follows Jesus
Acts 16

Supplies

- "We're Here!" Bible song (p. 202)
- short chain about 12" long (1 per child)
- plastic containers with lids or small potato chip cans with lids (1 per child)

Directions

Before class place one chain inside each container and attach the lid. Tape around the lids so that the children cannot pull the chains out of the containers.

During class talk with the children about how Paul and Silas were chained when they were in prison and about how their chains fell off when God sent the earthquake while they were singing.

Give each child a container with a chain inside. Teach the children the Bible song "We're Here!" Show the children how to keep a steady beat with the song by shaking their containers with the chains inside.

For a variation on this song, sing the verses and have the children join in on the chorus only.

Paul Tells about Jesus

Paul Helps People Follow Jesus

Acts 28; Ephesians 4, 6; Philippians 1–2; Colossians 4

Tune: "The Eensy Weensy Spider"

Walking or even riding a donkey,
or sailing on the waves across the deep blue sea,
Paul told of Jesus to everyone he found,
going to big cities and to little towns.

In the marketplace or from a prison cell,
Paul spoke of Jesus, bravely he did tell.
He taught the palace guards and in letters that he wrote.
He boldly told of Jesus with words and in his notes.

Always be humble, gentle, kind, and good.
Try to be patient as you know you should.
Be loving and forgiving every single day.
Ask God to help you daily when you stop to pray.

Following Footstep

Paul Helps People Follow Jesus
Acts 28; Ephesians 4, 6; Philippians 1–2; Colossians 4

These fun footprints remind kids to follow Jesus and to help others do the same!

Supplies

- construction paper (1 sheet per child)
- washable markers
- scissors
- hole punch
- yarn

Directions

Assign each child a partner in the class and give each child a piece of construction paper and a marker. One child in each pair should trace the outline of the other child's foot on the construction paper using a washable marker. Children can take their shoes off or leave them on for this activity. After one child has traced the other's foot, the children should exchange places so that the other child can also have a turn to trace.

Once each child has a foot traced on his paper, children should cut out the footprints and color them using washable markers. After children finish coloring, punch a hole in the heel of each footprint and tie a piece of yarn through the hole so that the footprints can be hung or dangled. Encourage children to write Jesus on their footprints.

Talk with the children about Paul's travels. Talk about the many places he went and about how he probably walked a long distance to tell others about Jesus. Remind the children that Paul helped others follow Jesus.

Allow the children to take their following footsteps home as reminders that we can tell others about Jesus, just like Paul did.

Option for Younger Children

For a class of younger children, before class you may want to cut out several footprints using a pattern. Allow the children to color the footprints in class.

All through the Night

A-Tisket, A-Tasket

Billy Boy

Clementine

Did You Ever See a Lassie?

Froggie Went a-Courtin'

Go Tell Aunt Rhody

I See the Moon

Little Liza Jane

Looby Lou

Make New Friends

Old King Cole

O Suzannah

Reuben and Rachel

God Cares

for ____________

David's Table, page 64
Esther Crowns, page 94

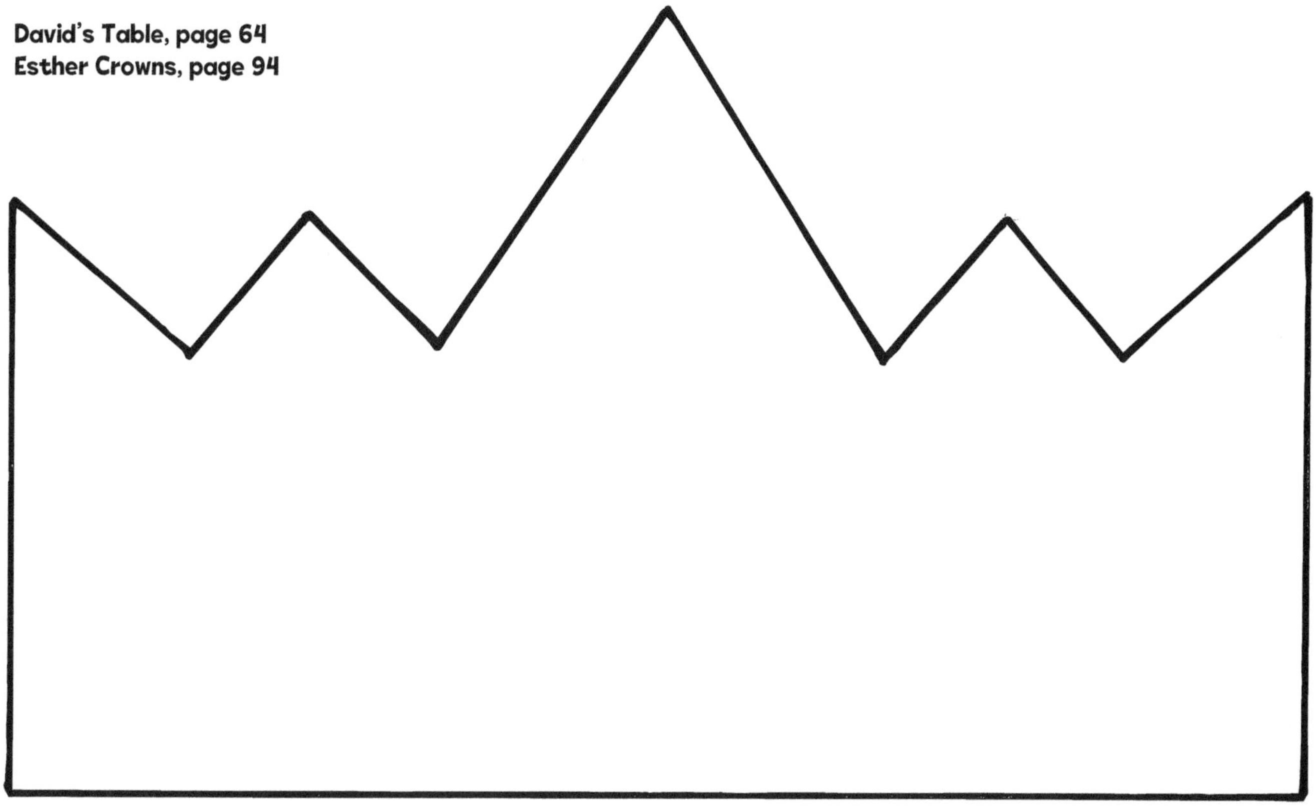

Feathers and Bread Raven, page 72

Sharing Hands, page 82

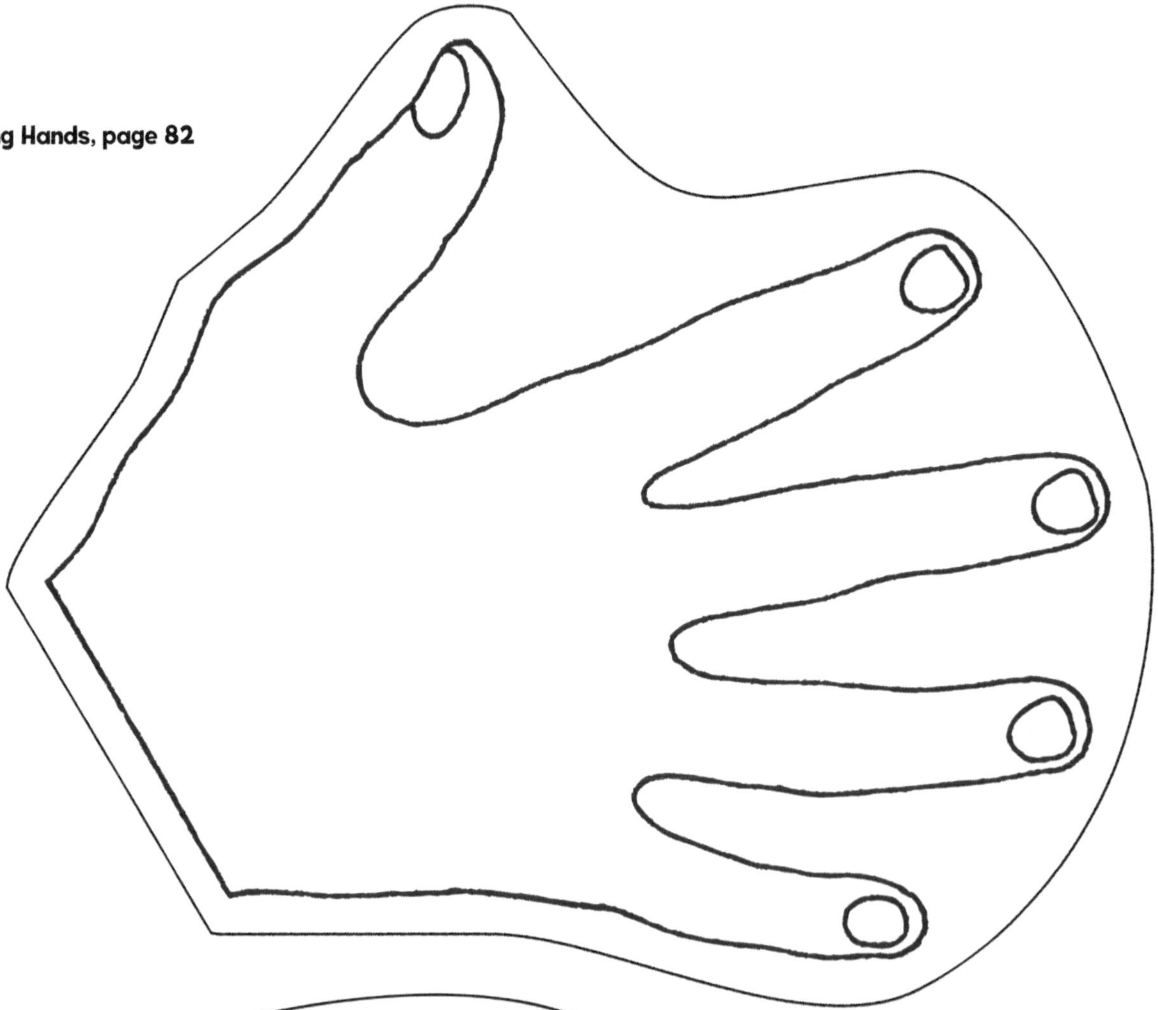

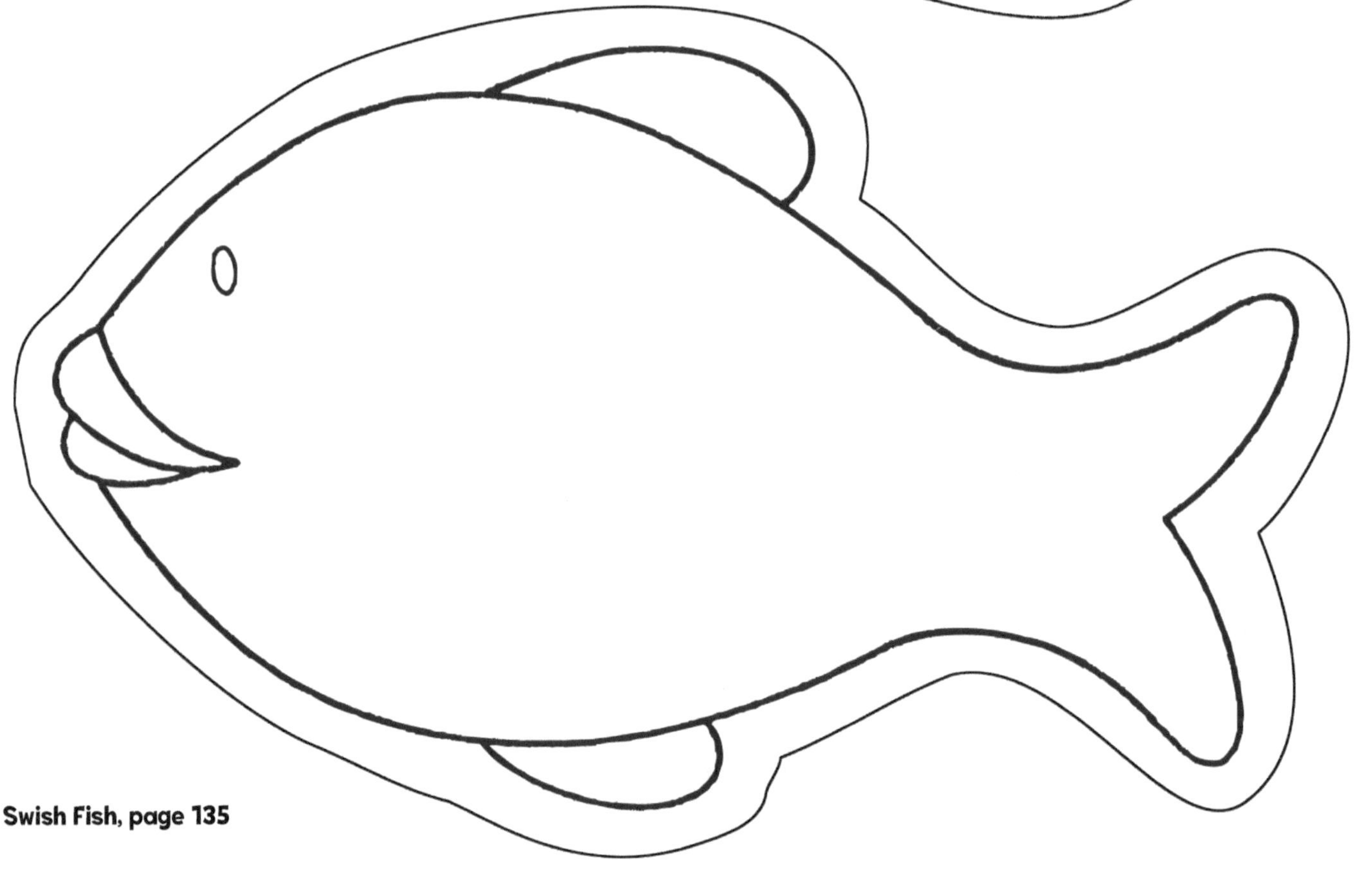

Swish Fish, page 135

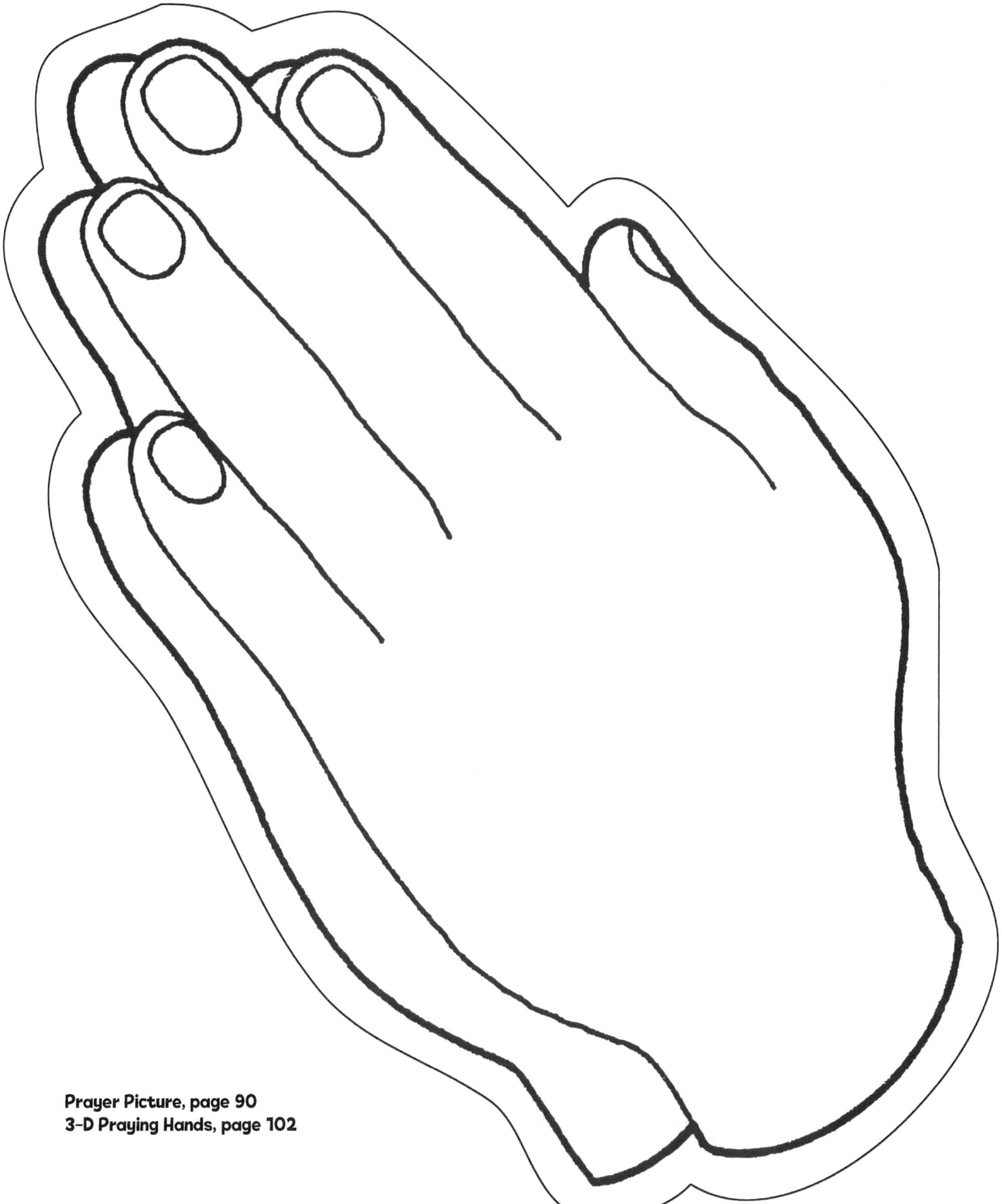

Prayer Picture, page 90
3-D Praying Hands, page 102

Star Chain, page 110

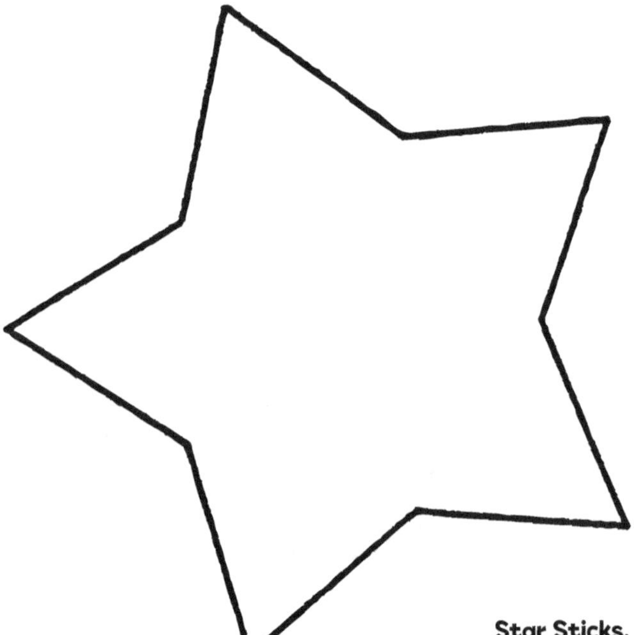

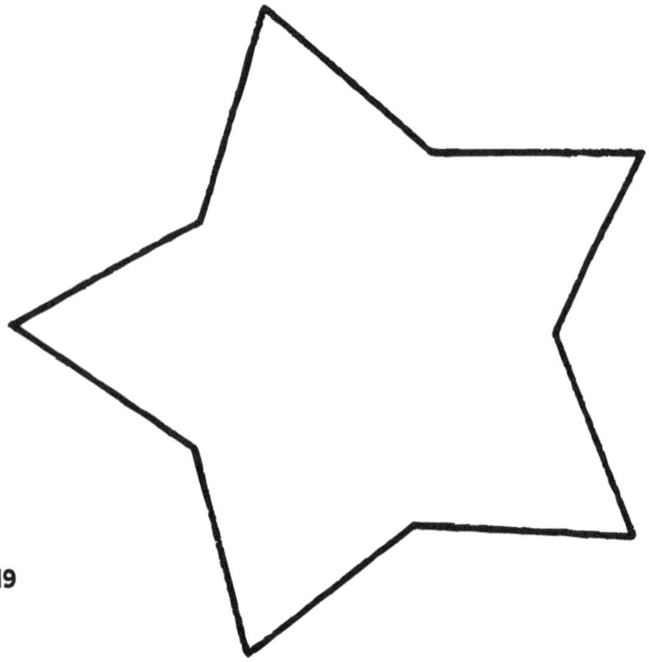

Star Sticks, page 119

Candy Cane Message, page 112

esus

is

God's

Son

Day and Night Stick Puppets, page 68

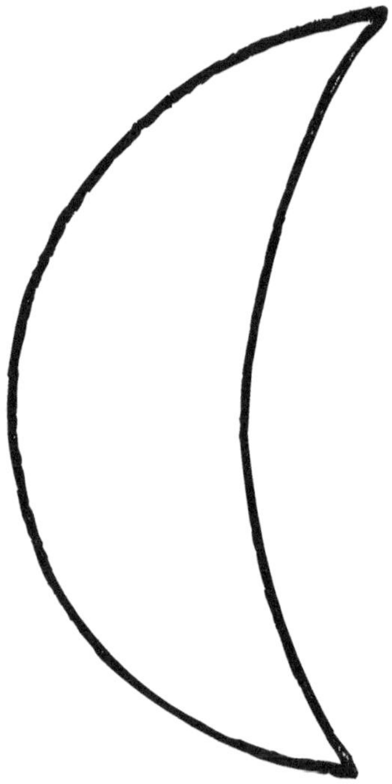

Footprint Follow, page 175
Stage a Stanza, page 197

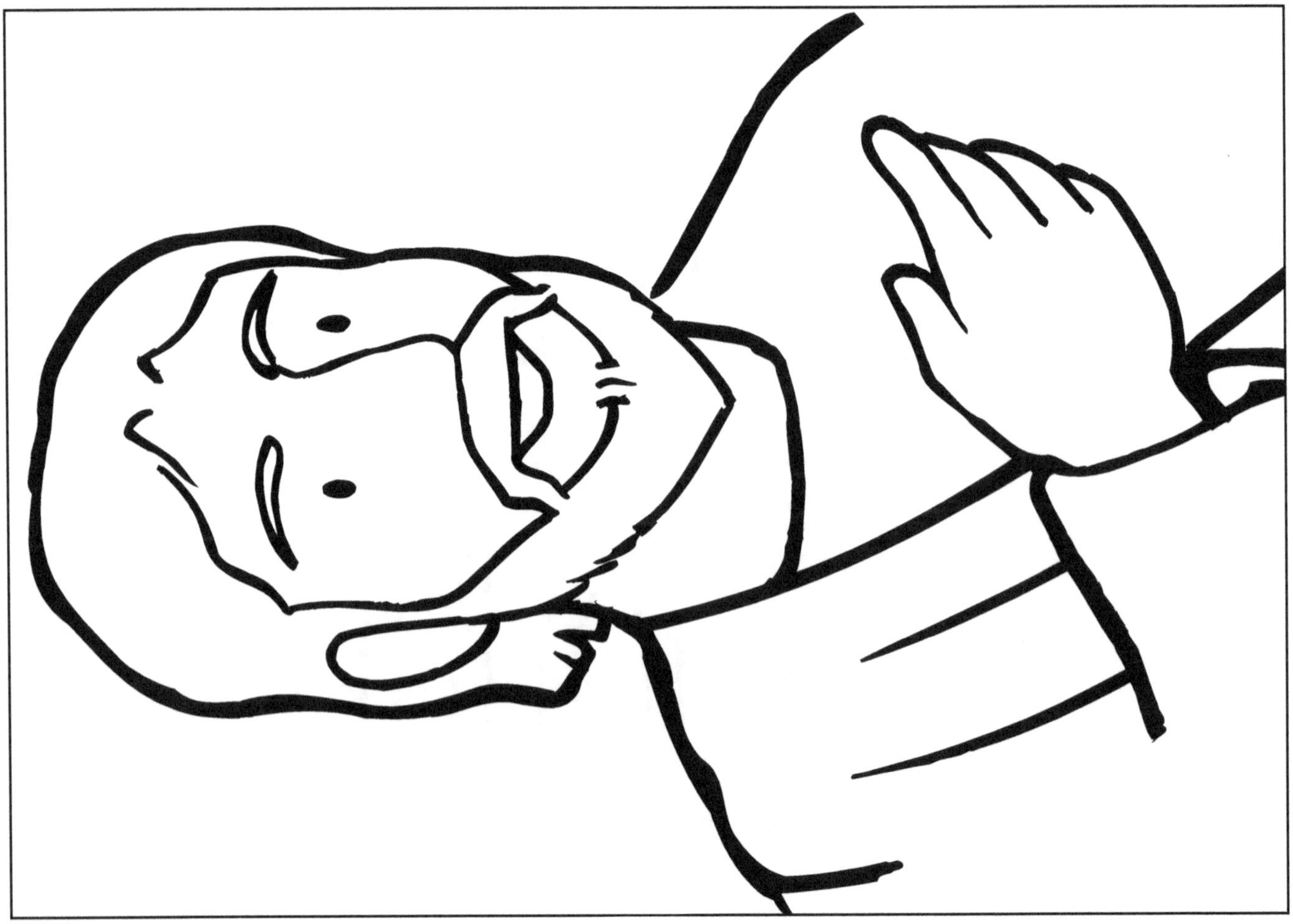

Looking for Jesus Scopes, page 121
Rap and Roll, page 137

Bag of Miracles, page 145

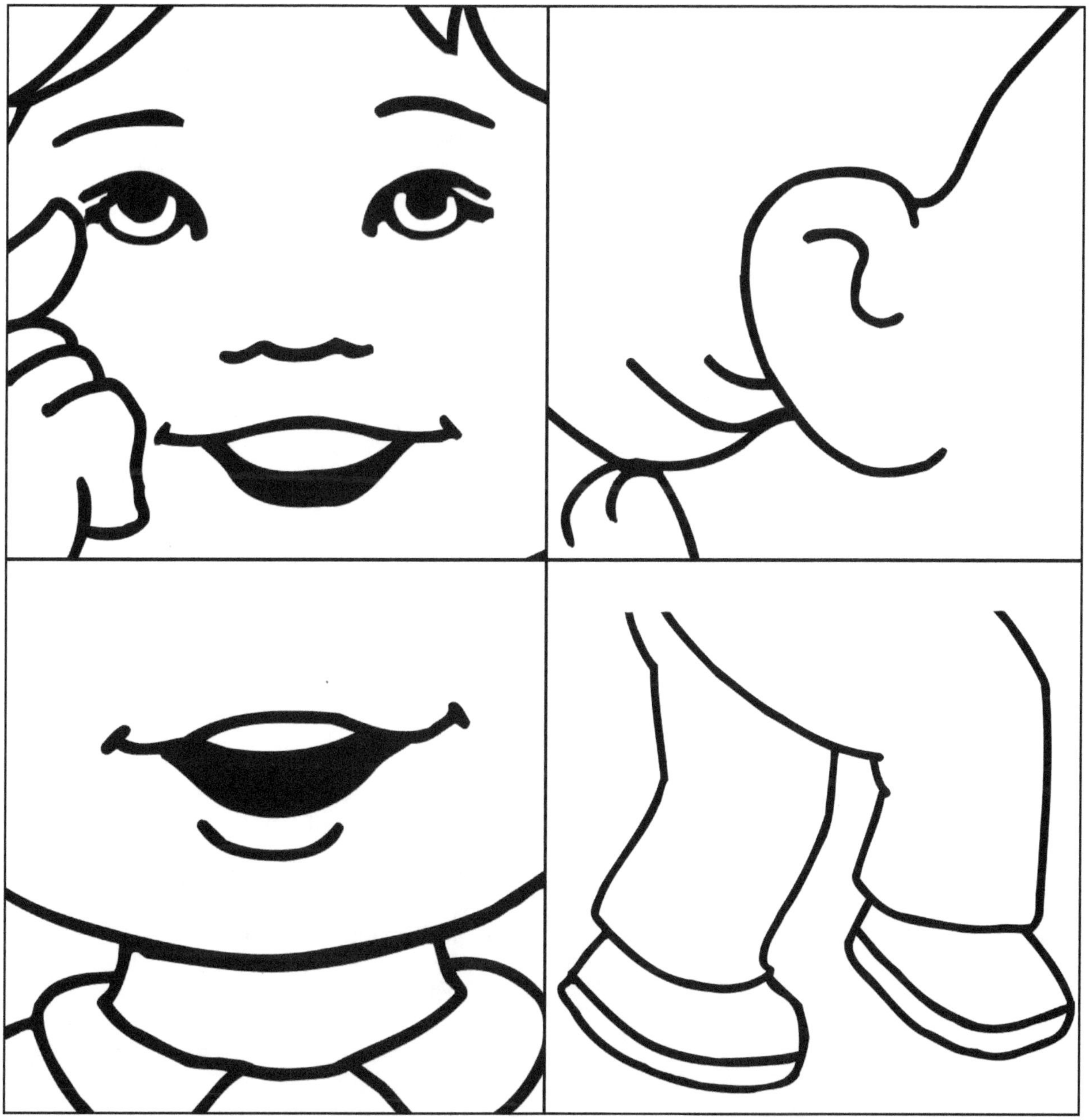

Index

Action Rhymes

Bible Songs

Teaching Ideas

HeartShaper
Shaping Hearts with God's Word

Preschool/Pre-K & K Scope & Sequence

Fall Year 1
- God Made the Sky and Earth (pp. 7–10)
- God Made Fish and Birds (pp. 7–10)
- God Made Animals (pp. 7–10)
- God Made People (pp. 11–13)
- Noah Builds a Boat (pp. 18–20)
- Noah and the Flood (pp. 18–20)
- Abram Moves (pp. 21–22)
- Abram and Lot (pp. 23–24)
- Abraham and Sarah Have a Baby (pp. 25–26)
- Joseph as a Boy (pp. 27–28)
- Joseph Serves God All His Life (pp. 29–30)
- Samuel as a Boy (pp. 53–54)
- Samuel Serves God All His Life (pp. 55–56)

Winter Year 1
- An Angel Announces Jesus' Birth (pp. 105–107)
- Jesus Is Born (pp. 108–110)
- Shepherds Visit Jesus (pp. 111–113)
- Simeon and Anna See Jesus (pp. 114–115)
- Wise Men Worship Jesus (pp. 116–119)
- Jesus as a Boy (pp. 120–121)
- Jesus Is Baptized (pp. 122–123)
- Jesus Is Tempted (pp. 124–125)
- Jesus Begins to Teach (pp. 132–133)
- Jesus and the Children (pp. 172–173)
- Jesus and Matthew (pp. 138–139)
- Jesus and a Woman from Samaria (pp. 128–129)
- Jesus and Zacchaeus (pp. 176–177)

Spring Year 1
- *People Praise Jesus (pp. 180–181)
- *Jesus Lives! (pp. 184–185)
- Jesus Heals an Official's Son (pp. 130–131)
- Jesus Heals a Man Who Could Not Walk (pp. 136–137)
- Jesus Heals the Soldier's Servant (pp. 144–145)
- Jesus Brings a Young Man Back to Life (pp. 146–147)
- Jesus Walks on Water (pp. 154–155)
- Jesus Heals a Man Who Could Not Hear or Speak (pp. 156–157)
- Peter Preaches about Jesus (pp. 186–187)
- Peter and John at the Temple (pp. 190–191)
- Phillip Tells about Jesus (pp. 192–193)
- Peter and Tabitha (pp. 196–197)
- The Church Prays for Peter in Prison (pp. 198–199)

Summer Year 1
- David Plays for Saul (pp. 57–58)
- David Meets Goliath (pp. 59–60)
- David and Jonathan (pp. 61–62)
- David and Mephibosheth (pp. 63–64)
- David Sings to God (pp. 65–66)
- Solomon Prays to Know What Is Right (pp. 67–68)
- Solomon Builds the Temple (pp. 69–70)
- Jehoshaphat Asks for God's Help (pp. 89–90)
- Josiah Reads God's Word (pp. 87–88)
- Elisha and a Widow's Oil (pp. 79–80)
- Elisha and a Shunammite Family (pp. 81–82)
- Elisha and the Shunammite's Son (pp. 83–84)
- Elisha and Naaman (pp. 85–86)

Fall Year 2

- God Made a World for People (pp. 7–10)
- God Made Adam and Eve (pp. 11–13)
- God Made My Senses (pp. 14–15)
- God Made Me Special (pp. 16–17)
- Moses Is Born (pp. 31–32)
- Moses Leads God's People (pp. 33–34)
- God's People Cross the Red Sea (pp. 35–36)
- God Provides for His People (pp. 37–38)
- God Gives Ten Rules (pp. 39–40)
- Joshua and Caleb (pp. 41–42)
- God's People Cross the Jordan River (pp. 43–44)
- The Fall of Jericho (pp. 45–46)
- Joshua Talks to God's People (pp. 47–48)

Winter Year 2

- An Angel Brings Special News (pp. 105–107)
- A Special Baby Is Born (pp. 108–110)
- Shepherds Hear Special News (pp. 111–113)
- Wise Men Worship a Special Baby (pp. 116–119)
- Jesus Teaches about Pleasing God (pp. 140–141)
- Jesus Teaches about Giving (pp. 142–143)
- Jesus Teaches about Praying (pp. 164–165)
- Jesus Teaches about Helping (pp. 160–161)
- Jesus Teaches about Sharing (pp. 166–167)
- Two Friends Follow Jesus (pp. 126–127)
- Fishermen Follow Jesus (pp. 134–135)
- Mary and Martha Follow Jesus (pp. 162–163)
- Bartimaeus Follows Jesus (pp. 174–175)

Spring Year 2

- *A Crowd Welcomes Jesus (pp. 178–179)
- *Jesus Is Alive (pp. 182–183)
- Jesus Stops a Storm (pp. 148–149)
- Jesus Heals a Young Girl (pp. 150–151)
- Jesus Feeds a Crowd (pp. 152–153)
- Jesus Heals a Man Born Blind (pp. 158–159)
- Jesus Heals Ten Men (pp. 170–171)
- Jesus Brings Lazarus Back to Life (pp. 168–169)
- The Church Follows Jesus (pp. 188–189)
- Saul Begins to Follow Jesus (pp. 194–195)
- Lydia Follows Jesus (pp. 200–201)
- The Jailer Follows Jesus (pp. 202–203)
- Paul Helps People Follow Jesus (pp. 204–205)

Summer Year 2

- Elijah Is Fed by Ravens (pp. 71–72)
- Elijah Helps a Widow (pp. 73–74)
- Elijah Helps a Widow's Son (pp. 75–76)
- Elijah and the Prophets of Baal (pp. 77–78)
- Daniel and His Friends Obey God (pp. 95–96)
- Daniel's Friends Worship Only God (pp. 97–98)
- Daniel and the Handwriting on the Wall (pp. 99–100)
- Daniel and the Lions' Den (pp. 101–102)
- Gideon Lead's God's Army (pp. 49–50)
- Ruth Makes Good Choices (pp. 51–52)
- Jonah Tells about God (pp. 103–104)
- Esther Helps God's People (pp. 93–94)
- Nehemiah Rebuilds the Wall (pp. 91–92)